Si.

The Women Who Married, Lived, and Died for Henry VIII

By Michael W. Simmons

Table of Contents

Chapter One: Katherine of Aragon Princess of Spain and Queen of England (1509-1531)

The Princess of Wales

In March of 1489, Prince Arthur, son of Henry VII, the first Tudor monarch of England, was formally betrothed to the Infanta Catalina, youngest of the four daughters of Queen Isabella of Castile and King Ferdinand of Aragon. It was considered a most advantageous match for the two-year old English prince: Ferdinand and Isabella, both sovereign rulers in their own right, had united the smaller Spanish kingdoms into a single nation, and under their joint rule Spain had become one of the two most powerful political entities in Europe, vying for supremacy with France. Henry VII of England, by contrast, was a usurper who had killed the legitimate English king, Richard III, last of the Plantagenets, at the Battle of Bosworth, and his claim to the throne was considered dubious at best. The tiny princess he was courting on behalf of his son had a better right by blood to the throne of England than he did. Marrying his young son to the Spanish princess would thus immeasurably strengthen the position of both Henry and his dynasty. The heir of their union would be able to claim legitimate descent from the English royal house through both of his or her parents, and politically unstable England would make an important alliance with a powerful nation. The alliance seemed a natural move, as both England and Spain claimed France as a common enemy. Ferdinand was initially reluctant to send his daughter to England—it was uncertain whether she would be safe there, since only time would tell whether Henry VII would be able to keep his throne—but at the time, he was in sore need of military aid against the French, and in the end he agreed to contract a marriage between his three-year old daughter and Henry's son in exchange for this assistance.

Catalina—Katherine, as she would be known in England—was the daughter of a remarkable woman. Isabella of Spain gave birth to her most famous daughter in the midst of a war, after riding on horseback all day, and took only a few hours' rest before getting back in the saddle. It was Isabella of Spain who financed Christopher Columbus's voyages to the New World. She was descended from the oldest royal dynasties in Europe, and autocratic privilege ran deep in her blood. Her daughter Katherine was said to resemble Isabella the most out of all her children, in both looks and character. Isabella saw to it that her daughter received a good education by the standards of female learning before the Reformation. Katherine's tutor, a priest by the name of Alessandro Geraldini, remained close to her throughout her life, and accompanied her to England as her chaplain when she married.

It is important to consider the impact that Isabella had on Katherine's character when studying her marriage to Henry VIII and her behavior throughout the famous annulment suit that created a new religion and plunged England into decades of bloody religious conflict. In the late fifteenth and early sixteenth centuries, few girls, even if they were princesses, had a role model like Isabella of Spain. It was an age in which the mental, spiritual, physical, and social inferiority of women to men was taken for granted by everyone. Girls were the property of their parents; women were the property of their husbands until they were widowed, after which they were controlled by their husbands' families. This was the case in every class of society, from the poorest peasants to the peak of royalty. Complete submission and obedience to fathers and husbands was considered the spiritual, social, and legal duty of all women. Women were expected to be completely malleable to their husbands' desires, to the very fabric of their character and disposition of their mind. Men were raised in the expectation that, when they married, they would be entitled to dispose of their wives as they saw fit. If their wives displeased them in any way, they were legally permitted to turn them out of the house with nothing but the bare minimum of clothing to cover their nakedness. A princess was no less the property of her husband and family than was a poor woman. In fact, the expectation of complete submission was even greater for a queen, since her husband was not merely her lord, but lord of all the land.

The sole and incomplete exception to this system of female subjection and submission was the vanishingly rare instance in which a woman of royal birth happened to succeed to the throne and become sovereign ruler of her country. Assumptions about female inferiority of mind and spirit were not discarded in such cases, but since they conflicted with equally ingrained assumptions about royal exceptionalism and the divine right of kings, sovereign queens occupied a liminal space that some navigated poorly, and others used to transform their age and their country. Simply put, queens like Isabella of Spain, and later Elizabeth I of England, possessed the very rarest of all female commodities: agency. And though, as a queen consort, Katherine of Aragon did not possess anything like as much power and agency as her sovereign mother, Isabella set her daughter the example of a woman who did not give way to men in all things.

There were few women in Katherine's time who would have possessed the strength to oppose her husband's wishes as Katherine opposed Henry VIII's for so long; the fact that she was capable of doing so must owe something to the fact that she was her mother's daughter, and had learned the courage of conviction from her. That a woman might be right where a man was wrong, that she might find herself in a position where her duty to God compelled her to separate herself from the interests of her husband and her king, was an idea that would scarcely occur to many of Katherine's contemporaries. But it was Katherine's beliefs, as much as Henry VIII's obsession with having a son, that shook Europe and set England on the path to Reformation.

Katherine's crossing to England did not take place until 1501, when she was sixteen. When the princess and her large, lavishly furnished Spanish household arrived in England at last, she found that her future father-in-law had arranged a lavish reception for her. She was greeted by throngs of cheering people when her ship made port in Plymouth, and a gentleman of her cortege wrote to Isabella that she "could not have been received with greater joy than if she had been the savior of the world." From there, she made her way to London, and King Henry and Prince Arthur rode out to meet her. Though the king and the prince arrived after Katherine had already gone to bed, Henry insisted that she be awakened; he had never seen her in person, and he was deeply anxious to set eyes on her, to be sure that she was just as attractive and healthy as his own ambassadors and the Spanish portrait painters had led him to believe. He was not disappointed. Katherine was small and plump with pretty features, waist-length reddish gold hair, and a fair complexion. After Katherine and Arthur met the next day, the prince remarked that he "had never felt so much joy in his life as when he beheld the sweet face of his bride." It is unknown what Katherine felt when she saw her intended bridegroom.

Katherine and Arthur were married two days after Katherine's arrival in England, in full view of the English public—Henry VII had commissioned a special platform to be built so that the marriage could take place before the eyes of the people. Both bride and groom were clad in white satin, and the bride was given away by none other than the groom's ten-year old brother, Prince Henry, the Duke of York. After the ceremony, and the banquets, music, and dancing that followed, Katherine and Arthur were publicly "put to bed"—that is, led in their nightgowns by their attendants to a specially prepared wedding chamber, where they climbed under the covers, heard a prayer and a blessing by the Archbishop of Canterbury and the Bishop of London, and endured both lewd jokes and good wishes from friends and family, until at last the curtains were drawn around the bed and they were left alone to consummate the marriage.

What followed was what historian Alison Weir refers to as "one of the most controversial wedding-nights in history". In twenty-seven years' time, Katherine would testify under oath that she and her fifteen-year old husband never had sex: not on the wedding night, not once during their brief marriage. She was consistent on this point throughout her lifetime, never deviating from her story even under the most immense pressure. When Arthur died six months later, Katherine told everyone that she was still a virgin and that she had only slept in Arthur's bed some six or seven nights the whole time they were married. Everyone believed her, including the Pope, or her subsequent marriage to Prince Henry would never have been permitted. No one ever cast doubt on her story, until Henry VIII sued for annulment almost three decades later.

In December of 1501, about a month after their marriage, the newly married Prince and Princess of Wales traveled to Ludlow Castle in Wales so that Arthur could learn the art of government from a stable of carefully selected advisors and government officials. In March of 1502, both Katherine and Arthur became very ill with sweating sickness. No one is certain today what sweating sickness was, but in the 16th century it killed large numbers of people in England every spring and summer. Katherine recovered quickly, but Arthur, who had not been in good health when he married and had only been getting weaker since, died on April 2nd.

King Henry was distraught: first, for the death of his eldest and most beloved son, second, because Ferdinand of Spain was now demanding that Katherine be returned to her home country, along with the first installment of her massive dowry. This was a ploy—what Ferdinand really wanted was for Katherine to marry Arthur's brother Henry, who was eleven years old and now heir to the throne of England. Henry VII wanted this as well, but there was a serious obstacle to the marriage: Scripture forbids a man to marry his brother's wife. Katherine's marriage to Arthur placed her in the forbidden "degrees of affinity" to Henry, meaning that a papal dispensation would be necessary before the marriage could take place. It was highly likely that the Pope would be willing to grant this dispensation, provided that Katherine was still a virgin. Inquiries were made—delicately at first, then bluntly. The king asked Katherine to her face whether her marriage to Arthur had ever been consummated, while her Spanish chaperone interrogated Katherine's ladies in waiting and her laundresses. Katherine asserted that no consummation had taken place, and the investigation corroborated her claim.

During the negotiations for the second marriage, Henry's queen and Katherine's mother in law, Elizabeth of York, died after giving birth to her eighth child. The king mourned her deeply and sincerely, but soon he began to consider remarriage. He had only one son left; if anything should happen to the last remaining Tudor prince, another civil war might break out. It occurred to Henry then that that, rather than marrying the sixteen-year old Katherine to his eleven-year old son, he might marry Katherine himself. Ferdinand and Isabella, however, were appalled by the suggestion. Such a marriage was "a thing not to be endured". If Henry did not put it out of his mind, they would demand the return of Katherine and her dowry, and Henry could take his chances finding a bride for his son in France. Henry backed down, and Katherine spent the next four years living the life of a widow, waiting until her husband's brother grew old enough to consummate a marriage.

Prince Henry

Katherine must have had misgivings about being married to a child when she herself was nearing adulthood, but she was extremely fond of Prince Henry, and he of her. The recent death of his mother had aroused Katherine's protective instincts towards the young boy, and he had been nursing a childish crush towards her since her arrival in England. It was the beginning of a strong relationship full of mutual affection and respect which would last for decades, until it ended in catastrophe.

The future King Henry VIII was born in 1491, his parents' third child and second son. Apart from Arthur, he had an older sister, Margaret, who would one day marry James IV of Scotland. Of his five younger siblings, only his sister Mary would survive infancy, and Henry would entail the succession after his own children on her male descendants. As a boy, Henry had an excellent education along classical lines, studying Homer, Virgil, Plautus, Ovid, Thucydides, Livy, Pliny, and other Greek and Roman authors. He also studied mathematics, music, and French. Even as a young child, Henry was said to be charismatic, possessing "something of royalty in his demeanor, in which there was a certain dignity combined with singular courtesy." After Arthur's death, Henry's father grew deeply fearful that he would lose his last remaining son, and as a consequence Henry spent most of his time in his own suite of rooms, the only door of which led directly into his father's chambers. The years before his marriage to Katherine were probably as dreary for him as they were for her.

Pope Julius II, after some inward debate, granted the Bull of Dispensation permitting Katherine and Henry's marriage in December of 1503. The marriage was scheduled to take place in 1505, when Henry was fourteen. But then, in November of 1504, Katherine's fate was thrown into uncertainty: her mother, Isabella of Castile, died, and suddenly King Henry was no longer so impatient for Katherine to marry his son.

Practically speaking, a united Spain no longer existed. The heir to the kingdom of Castile was not Isabella's husband, Ferdinand, but their daughter, Katherine's sister Juana. This meant that when Katherine and Henry married, England would have an alliance with Ferdinand's kingdom of Aragon, but not with the united kingdoms of Aragon and Castile.

Overnight, Katherine's status in the world plummeted, and King Henry's behavior towards her grew markedly colder. He ceased giving her an allowance, which meant that she had no money to pay her servants, maintain her wardrobe, or even buy food. And although the formal marriage contract between Katherine and Henry lacked nothing but the act of consummation to be a legally binding union, the king determined that he would cancel the marriage if he could arrange a better match for his son behind Ferdinand's back. Furthermore, on the day before Prince Henry's fourteenth birthday, the king secretly took him before the Bishop of Winchester and "made the boy solemnly revoke the promises made at his betrothal, on the grounds that they were made when he was a minor and incapable under the law of deciding such things for himself." In light of how his marriage to Katherine ended, it can only be wondered what sort of psychological impact this rough ceremony had on the young Henry's conception of the relationship between politics and marriage.

Katherine passed her years of widowhood in despair, genteel poverty, and anxiety while her father, King Henry, and various ambassadors conducted politics around her. For much of this time, Katherine was convinced that her marriage to Prince Henry would never take place. Though her status in the court improved somewhat after Ferdinand appointed her his ambassador to the English court—making her the first woman in European history to receive such a distinction—it was not until Henry VII was dying of consumption that he finally made up his mind to permit the marriage. By this time, Prince Henry was seventeen, and the king's advisors felt it was high time that he get down to the business of producing heirs for the succession. The king himself, knowing that he was shortly to account to God for his actions, felt troubled in his conscience over his miserly, ungracious behavior towards Katherine, and he wanted his son to make it up to her.

Over the years, Prince Henry had sometimes behaved towards Katherine with great affection, and at other times ignored her entirely, depending on whether his father was feeling favorably disposed towards the marriage or not. Still, when the king told Henry, on his deathbed, to honor the marriage contract with Katherine, the prince found the command perfectly agreeable. He had only one objection. Katherine had been his brother's wife, and this troubled his conscience, despite the fact that the Pope had given his blessing. But did the Pope have the authority to countermand the express command of Scripture? This misgiving, which Henry found relatively easy to overcome as a teenager, would return to trouble him later in life.

The newly crowned king Henry VIII and the long-suffering Spanish princess Katherine of Aragon were married at long last on June 11, 1509. The ceremony took place in Katherine's private rooms, presided over by the Archbishop of Canterbury. It was followed by a private mass and a private wedding night. Katherine felt that all her prayers had been answered. Our lingering image of the historical Henry tends to be informed by his appearance at the end of his life, when he was sick, miserable, and so fat that it was said that four large men could fit into his doublet. But the young Henry VIII was considered one of the handsomest men of his court. He was extraordinarily tall for a man of his time, standing between 6'2 and 6'4. It is not uncommon for reports of a king's appearance to be unduly flattering, but Henry's skeleton was discovered intact in the 19th century, and it was found to measure 6'2, while his armor was made to fit a man an inch or so taller. He was athletic and fit in his youth, with the same fair skin and reddish hair that his daughter Elizabeth would later be famous for. "His Majesty is the handsomest potentate I ever set eyes on," wrote a contemporary observer, who added that he had "a round face so beautiful that it would become a pretty woman... Nature could not have done more for him. He is very fair, his whole frame admirably proportioned."

In addition to all this, Henry was highly intelligent, scholarly, and charismatic, "the most gentle and affable prince in the world." His observational skills, general knowledge, and reasoning abilities were profound, and his courtiers found him to be an intellectual "with most piercing talents". He did have his faults; one historian characterizes him as "quick-tempered, headstrong, immature, and vain." But on the whole, our opinion of Henry VIII tends to be so soured by the unpleasant drama of his six marriages that it is easy to forget his better qualities. The fact of the matter was, in 1509, Katherine was marrying the most eligible and desirable of all possible bridegrooms. No one was allowed to remain in doubt that this marriage had been consummated immediately.

One of Henry VIII's chief interests was theology, and in 1521, while recovering from an illness, he completed a work entitled *In Defense of the Seven Sacraments*. Written in Latin, and assisted somewhat by his advisor Sir Thomas More, this treatise made a point by point refutation of the heresies of Martin Luther, who claimed that of the seven sacraments celebrated by the Roman Catholic church, only two were theologically validated by Scripture. Henry wrote on each of the sacraments in turn, treating Luther's reasoning with sneering contempt, and explaining at length why each of the sacraments deserved to be honored as such. The pope was in raptures over this work of theological scholarship and rewarded Henry with the title "Defender of the Faith". Ironically, the kings and queens of England bear this title to the present day, despite the fact that England became Protestant a few decades later and has remained so ever since. In this treatise, Henry waxed particularly eloquent in defense of the sacrament of marriage:

"O Word as full of Joy and Fears as it is of Admiration! Who should not rejoice, that God has so much Care over his Marriage, as to vouchsafe, not only to be present at it, but also to preside in it? Who should not tremble, while he is in Doubt how to use his Wife, whom he is not only bound to love, but also to live with, in such as Manner, as that he may be able to render her pure and immaculate to God, from whom he has received her?"

It is impossible to read such an impassioned testimony today without being conscious of the irony. Not only would Henry, Defender of the Faith, break the supremacy of the Roman Catholic church forever within a couple of decades of publishing this work, but there is a certain poignancy in the way he reiterates that "whom God has joined together, let no Man put asunder." He would "join" with six women over the course of his lifetime, and he himself would sunder his connection with four of them.

Katherine, Queen of England

When Katherine married Henry, she assumed a new role and identity. She was mother to the people of her adopted country, and soon, it was to be hoped, she would be the mother of Henry's children. After her marriage, she adopted the motto "Humble and Loyal" and took as her badge the pomegranate, a symbol of fertility; these words and this image would adorn her linens, her plate, etc. She was twenty-three years old, an age at which most women in the Tudor era were already mothers many times over; it was not uncommon for a girl to marry at 15 and have her first child nine months later. Yet there was no reason not to think she would be fertile, as her mother had given birth to ten children, and her sisters, even the mad one, all had healthy children.

As queen, she was much loved by all who knew her, from her people to her personal attendants. She adopted a humble and deferential manner, and to her dependents she was kind and courteous—those servants who had continued to serve her faithfully before her marriage even during the periods when she was unable to pay their salary were generously rewarded once she was Queen. Overall, she had an air of maturity which was perhaps heightened by the difference in her and Henry's ages. Her sister Juana, the mad queen of Castile whose kingdom had been taken over by their father Ferdinand, was prone to screaming tantrums and fits of melancholy, but these were not present in steady, faithful Katherine. Even in her love for Henry, she was moderate; her devotion ran deep, but it was not showy. When Queen Juana's husband Philip died she had refused to relinquish his corpse and pressed kisses to his decomposing face during the funeral; Katherine, by contrast, bore with the many sorrows, indignities, and disappointments of her life with composure and grace. The great humanist scholar Erasmus praised her to Henry, saying, "your wife spends that time in reading the sacred volume which other princesses occupy in cards and dice." Her piety and faith ran deep even in an age where religious observances were compulsory, and even if she was not as intelligent as the supremely gifted Henry, she was extremely well read in theology and scripture.

Henry and Katherine's sex life is of historical interest, in light of how and why their marriage ended. One historian describes the elaborate ritual that attended their couplings:

"Traditionally, kings and queens had separate apartments in the royal palaces. If the King wished to sleep with his wife at night—a matter of public interest, since the succession must be assured—he went in procession, escorted to her chamber door by members of his guard and gentlemen of his privy chamber. Katherine, in turn, having been undressed by her ladies, would be sitting up in the great tester bed waiting for him. On the nights the King did not honor her with his company, a maid would occupy a truckle bed at the foot of her bed, but she was banished whenever the King arrived unannounced, as he often did. Then his guards would be posted outside the doors to the Queen's apartments. Henry VIII was very sensitive about security, and any bed he slept in was always made up by his servants, according to an elaborate ritual which involved a sword being thrust between the mattress and the feather bed, just in case an intruder had secreted himself there."

There is no doubt that Henry loved Katherine. He was a passionate subscriber to the cult of chivalry and courtly love, in which men of noble worth took it as their duty to defend helpless women. The fact that he had, by marrying her, been able to save Katherine from the poverty and neglect she had endured after his brother's death, made her a figure of romantic charm to him, if not passionate sexual attraction. Long after she lost the charms of her first youth and settled into matronly stolidity, Henry had deep affection and genuine respect for her, heightened by her submissive, grateful manner towards him. He had every reason to think that God had blessed him with the best of wives—until, gradually, old fears began to haunt him.

Children

Within a year of their marriage, Katherine was pregnant. It ended nine months later in the birth of a stillborn daughter, and Katherine was devastated. The child was both female and dead—the latter was only marginally more disappointing than the former. Henry, at least, accepted the news philosophically, since it was almost more common than not to lose a first child in this way, but Katherine was intensely depressed. Her one great duty in life was to provide her husband with children, sons first and foremost. Within a year she was pregnant again. During this second pregnancy, she discovered that Henry had begun to take mistresses, which upset her immensely. Henry was equally upset—he felt that Katherine had no right to interfere with his doing as he pleased, particularly as he had conducted the affair discreetly, without depriving Katherine of any of her rights as his wife (save, of course, the right to a faithful husband). When Katherine found that no one was on her side—everyone expected that wives should turn a blind eye to their husband's infidelities—she collected herself, and never again upbraided Henry for his affairs. But her pride had taken a considerable blow.

On January 1, 1511, Katherine gave birth to a son, who was named Henry. The King was beside himself with joy, and ordered months of public festivities to celebrate the prince's arrival. For a month and half, they were the happiest of families. Then, on February 22, Prince Henry died suddenly. It was a tremendous blow; he had not been ill, he had merely ceased to live between one moment and the next. Even now, the King was generous and gracious towards his wife. He was more worried about her mental health than he was about the death of his son, though he mourned deeply for the little prince and ordered a lavish state funeral for him at Westminster Abbey.

Katherine's fall from Henry's favor began gradually, and, at least at first, had little to do with their misfortunes as parents. Henry was, by the standards of his time, a man when he came to the throne, but he was also a teenager, and despite his prodigious abilities he naturally preferred hunting and jousting with his friends to dealing with state affairs. He was not a negligent ruler, but some areas of governance were more tedious than others, and in time he found himself relying increasingly upon the advice of an ambitious man who was more than happy to act as the power behind the throne: Cardinal Thomas Wolsey, once chaplain to Henry VII, who had taken pains to ingratiate himself with the young king upon his succession. Henry was impressed by Wolsey's counsel, but his influence over Henry was resented by many people at court, including Katherine. In the early years of their marriage, Henry was also deeply reliant on Katherine's advice, which his courtiers also resented, not so much because she was Spanish-born as because she considered it her duty to advance the interests of Spain, sometimes even over the interests of England. Wolsey, however, was pro-French in his foreign policy. Katherine neither liked nor trusted Wolsey, and he, in turn, began to resent her influence over the King.

In 1513, Katherine was pregnant again, and this pregnancy ended in the premature birth of a stillborn son. Their disappointment was again great, but in 1514 she was pregnant again. Katherine and Henry's relationship soured during the course of this pregnancy. He had recently gone to her father, King Ferdinand, asking for support in an attempt to depose the French king and assume the French throne for himself. Ferdinand had confounded his plans, and Henry returned to England full of bitterness against Katherine's father, bitterness which spilled over onto Katherine herself. This placed the Queen in an extremely delicate position; she had been raised to give unquestioning obedience to both her father and her husband, and now her father and husband were enemies. Katherine's friends, even those members of her household who had come to England with her from Spain, urged her not to advocate for her father's interests any longer, and Katherine agreed that this was the wisest course—between her husband and her father, her first loyalty must be to her husband. Nonetheless, Henry never again consulted her in political matters, and when her fourth pregnancy ended in the birth of another stillborn son, their relationship became more distant still.

Finally, in February of 1516, Katherine gave birth to the child who was destined to be the only living offspring of her marriage to Henry: Princess Mary, the future Queen Mary I. It was disappointing that she was not a boy, of course, but the King was delighted by her, calling her "a right lusty princess" on account of her loud cries. "If it is a daughter this time, by the grace of God, boys will follow," Henry remarked. "We are both still young." But he was wrong. Katherine's sixth and final pregnancy followed in 1518, and another girl was born—alive, but she died before her christening could take place three days later. Katherine was, by now, thirty-two years old. Women did have children in their thirties and even in their forties, but it was well known that the risks grew greater the older the mother was, and thirty-two was old by Tudor standards. Katherine could not help feeling sorrow; over the course of her nine-year marriage she had given birth six times, losing her figure, her beauty, and her youth in the process, and she had only one daughter to show for it.

In England, unlike some other European countries, a king's daughter could inherit his throne, but it had never happened before—in fact, Mary I was destined to become the very first queen regnant of England, followed shortly by her sister Elizabeth as the second queen. The idea of a female monarch made everyone uneasy, because she would inevitably marry, and it was thought that the man she married would inevitably be the true ruler of England. Both Mary and Elizabeth would, in different ways, prove these expectations wrong, but this did not change the fact that Mary's birth did nothing to allay people's fears that the succession was in jeopardy. And no one was more fearful on that account than the King himself.

As of 1519, Henry's lack of a male heir had become his most pressing worry. One of the king's most sacred duties was providing his people with a legitimate heir, so that upon his death there was no room for doubt into whose hands power would pass, no foothold for secret cabals of ambitious men to install a king of their choosing. Unlike his father, Henry VIII's legitimacy as King was never called into question. Henry VII had been a usurper, but his wife, Elizabeth of York, was beyond any dispute the rightful Plantagenet heiress, meaning that in the eyes of his people Henry VIII's reign represented a return to rule by the great English dynasty of old. But if Henry died without issue, there were other Plantagenets, all with strong blood claims to the English throne, who would seize the opportunity to regain power, even though it would mean civil war. Noblemen lost their heads and their lands during such wars, but the common people suffered on an even more profound level, and it was Henry's duty to protect them from such a fate.

As things stood, Princess Mary was the heir to the English throne, but in Henry's eyes, though he doted on her with all the love of a devoted father, a female heir was scarcely better than no heir at all. Quite apart from concerns about who she would marry, women were considered too weak to take and hold power. Despite Henry's good health, he might die at any moment, in battle, in a hunting accident, from the plagues that routinely swept the country—leaving a three-year old girl Queen of England. She might be deposed, even killed, and where would the succession be then? So convinced was Henry that Princess Mary could never be Queen in England that when she was three years old he attempted to contract a marriage for her that would one day make her queen consort of France, though this contract was later canceled.

Even though Katherine was considered old, she was not yet, biologically speaking, past her childbearing years when Henry ceased to visit her bed on a regular basis. He hinted that sexual relations with her had become distasteful to him, owing to "some gynecological trouble" that had resulted from her last pregnancy and lying in. In 1525, when Katherine turned forty, she was considered to be "past that age in which women most commonly are wont to be fruitful," meaning that she probably began menopause. Henry gave up all hope of her presenting him with any more children.

Fatefully for Katherine, another event occurred in 1519: her nephew Charles was elected Holy

Roman Emperor after the death of the old emperor, Maximilian. Not only did this elevate Katherine's status in England and abroad, it meant that, after her father King Ferdinand died, she would have a powerful ally and backer when, in the years to come, Henry sought to divorce her.

The Boleyns

In 1527, Henry began to experience a resurgence of his old doubts regarding the Scriptural validity of his marriage. He had been reading, and re-reading, the book of Leviticus, in which it is said that, "If a man shall take his brother's wife, it is an unclean thing; he hath uncovered his brother's nakedness; they shall be childless." This doctrinal issue had been debated to exhaustion long before the marriage took place, with various priests pointing out that the Scripture as a whole was not definitive; the book of Deuteronomy positively encouraged such marriages. But with Katherine now entering menopause, the doctrinal issue was assuming a larger importance in Henry's eyes. He was not childless, of course; there was Mary to think of. But to Henry, a female child was no child at all, not when the succession was in doubt.

In 1521, his mistress, Bessie Blount, had born him a son, Henry Fitzroy (Fitzroy means "son of the King") and Henry had brought the boy to court, loading him with noble titles and according him such honor that his courtiers began to suspect that Henry meant to legitimize him and attempt to instate him as his heir. This had never been attempted with a King's bastard before, and no one knew how such a move would be received. Henry obviously had doubts of his own, because he never made any formal move to legitimize Fitzroy. But by the late 1520's, he was sufficiently convinced that his marriage to Katherine was incestuous that he ceased all sexual relations with her.

Two more events took place in 1527 which combined to spur the King to his fateful decision to seek an annulment of his marriage to Katherine. The first was that conservative religious authorities, raising the incest issue, claimed that Princess Mary herself was not legitimate, because Henry's marriage to Katherine was not valid. This echoed the doubts which had been haunting Henry for years. And then, in the spring of that year, the final impetus for action arrived. The event which carried him over the precipice from doubt to certainty was a simple one: in 1527, for the first time in his life, Henry VIII fell passionately in love.

Chapter Two: Anne Boleyn and the King's Great Matter (1533-1536)

Mistress Anne

It is often assumed that Henry VIII's love affair with Anne Boleyn was, if not his sole motivation for divorcing his wife, breaking English ties with the Roman Catholic church, and igniting a century of religious warfare in his country, it was at least the event which prompted him to begin entertaining doubts about the validity of his marriage to Katherine. But as we have established, those doubts had been in existence long before he ever met her.

If Anne Boleyn had not been a woman of unusual intelligence, ambition, and perspicacity, it is likely that she would have undergone the same obscure fate as her sister Mary—that she would have become Henry's mistress, perhaps enjoying that unofficial but lucrative role for longer than her predecessors, only to retire in middle age with rich rewards for her service. But Anne distinguished herself from her sister in the most significant way possible: she refused to have sexual relations with Henry. She was no strumpet; she was a virtuous woman, one of the

Queen's own maids of honor, and she would not cheapen herself for any man, even the King. As one historian puts it, "she would have marriage, and the crown of England, or nothing." There is no doubt that her chastity both increased Henry's need to possess her, and made him see her as an appropriate replacement for Katherine as Queen. He would not, after all, have ever considered raising Bessie Blount or Mary Boleyn to that station.

There are several vital facts about Anne Boleyn that must be borne in mind when studying her life and her role in Henry VIII's "Great Matter": her ambition, intelligence, and devotion to the cause of church reform made her admirably suited to fight alongside Henry for the annulment. But these same qualities made her poorly suited to the role of Henry's queen. He fully expected that once she was married she would change herself to suit him—to be the kind of queen that Katherine had been, meek, submissive, rarely disagreeing with him. But marriage did not transform her into the ideal Tudor wife. She remained as she had always been, proud, unwilling to mend bridges or placate her enemies, and this, not the bizarre and fictitious crimes for which she was arrested, condemned, and executed—crimes that ranged from incest to witchcraft—were her undoing.

Anne was hated during her lifetime, both by simple people who regarded her as a homewrecker, and by Catholics who considered her responsible for the schism with Rome. Likewise, Protestants writing after her death, especially during the reign of her brilliant and famous daughter, considered Anne to be something like a saint. One of her earliest biographers wrote that "this princely lady was elect of God." Shakespeare, writing of Anne in his later play *Henry VIII,* depicted both her and the King as the innocent pawns of duplicitous politicians—a delicately managed trick, considering that Queen Elizabeth honored the memories of both her parents, despite the fact that her father had killed her mother, and James I, her successor, claimed descent from Henry on his mother's side. All in all, Anne Boleyn was neither the promiscuous, incestuous witch she was made out to be in her lifetime, nor was she a saint. She was, perhaps, born in the wrong time, or to the wrong station in life. Her daughter Elizabeth shared many of her qualities, but in an anointed sovereign, they were regarded as strengths.

The young Anne Boleyn

Of Henry VIII's six wives, four were commoners. Anne was the first of these. This made her only the second woman not of royal blood to marry an English king; the first had been Elizabeth Woodville, who had married Edward IV, brother of Richard III. Her mother, Elizabeth Howard, laid claim to ancient noble ancestry, but her father, Thomas Boleyn, came of the new merchant middle class. Thomas and Elizabeth had many children, but only Mary, Anne, and a brother, George, survived to adulthood. Anne was the middle child, but there is some dispute as to her exact date of birth; our best historical evidence suggests that she was born in 1500 or 1501, making her about thirty-five when she died. It is not even certain whether she or Mary was the eldest daughter, but circumstantial evidence suggests that Mary was the first born. George was indisputably the youngest of the three.

When Anne was a young child, probably eleven or twelve, her father placed her in the service of Margaret of Austria, Regent of the Netherlands, who made Anne one of her maids of honor. This position would have given Anne the sort of training and education that a future lady in waiting to the Queen of England needed. Margaret of Austria was evidently delighted with

Anne's companionship, for she wrote to Thomas Boleyn that Anne was,

"...a present more than welcome in my sight. I hope to treat her in such a way that you shall be quite satisfied with me. I find in her so fine a spirit, and so perfect an address for a lady of her years, that I am more beholden to you for sending her than you can be to me for receiving her."

At the Dutch court, Anne was instructed by a French governess named Simonette, and as a result of her tutelage Anne was fluent in French by the time she returned to England eighteen months later, where she became a maid of honor to Henry VIII's sister, Mary Tudor, then about to be married to Louis XII, King of France. Her sister Mary was also part of Mary Tudor's retinue. Shortly after the royal marriage, Louis sent most of Mary Tudor's maids back to England, but Anne and Mary Boleyn were permitted to remain. When Louis XII died abruptly in 1515, the Boleyn sisters continued to serve his widow until Mary Tudor returned to England and secretly married Charles Brandon, the Earl of Suffolk; Mary and Charles's granddaughter, Lady Jane Grey, would reign as Queen of England for nine days before being deposed by Mary I. The Boleyn sisters did not return to England with the Suffolks, however; Louis XII's successor, Francis I, invited them to remain as ladies in waiting to his wife, Claude of Valois, because they both spoke excellent French.

The court of Francis I was unusually licentious, with adultery and extramarital sexual affairs conducted so openly that they passed for a sport alongside hunting and jousting. Queen Claude, by contrast, was so pious that she lived apart from the royal court and ran her own household along the lines of a nunnery. She felt deep responsibility towards the young women who served her and was continually fearful lest the sexual opportunists in her husband's court would corrupt them. Mary Boleyn, it seems, fulfilled her worst fears, though ultimately it did her little harm. Anne, on the other hand, devoted herself to studying the Queen's stately manners. A French poet, observing Anne during this period of her life, wrote that, "She became so graceful that you would never have taken her for an Englishwoman, but for a Frenchwoman born." She became an icon of fashion in France, and when she returned to England she set fashions that would endure for decades after her death. She was considered too small and thin to be beautiful, and her sharp narrow features did not suit Tudor standards of prettiness in women, but she had a quick wit, lively manners, and an alluring charm that captivated men. However, one of Anne Boleyn's most famous physical qualities, the sixth finger on her left hand, is a mere invention of biographers. Instead, she had "a second nail upon the side of her nail upon one of her fingers"; far from using it to perform diabolical ceremonies, she was self-conscious about it and introduced a fashion for long sleeves on purpose to keep it hidden.

Anne Boleyn managed to complete her service to Claude of Valois early in 1522 with her reputation intact; none other than the whoremongering Francis I himself wrote to Thomas Boleyn that she was remarkable amongst his court for being "discreet and modest". Though Henry VIII would later claim that he had discovered her to have been "sexually corrupted" while in France, there is no telling what he meant by it. Certainly no hint of scandal was attached to her when she returned to England. She came back to England with such polish, grace, and poise that her father had no difficulty in quickly securing a place for her amongst Queen Katherine's ladies. And it was in this manner that Henry VIII first came to take serious notice of her.

Henry VIII courts Anne Boleyn

The story goes that during a Lenten pageant in March of 1522, less than two months after Anne and her sister came home to England, she was selected by the Master of the Revels to be one of the ten dancers, five male and five female, who emerged from "a model of a castle called the *Château Vert*" which had been wheeled into the banquet hall after dinner. Henry VIII was one of the male dancers, masked to conceal his identity; the female dancers, besides Anne, were her sister Mary, who was by then already Henry's mistress, along with Mary Tudor, the King's sister, and two other noblewomen. All the ladies were dressed in gowns of white satin embroidered with gold thread. Shakespeare depicts this dance as the moment in which Henry first began to fall in love with Anne, despite the fact that his historical affair with Anne would not begin for another five years. In the play, Henry chooses Anne as his partner for the dance, remarking to himself:

> "The fairest hand I ever touch'd! O beauty,
>
> Till now I never knew thee!"

After the dance, Henry inquires of the Lord Chamberlain concerning the identity of the lady he had danced with:

KING HENRY VIII

My lord chamberlain,

Prithee, come hither: what fair lady's that?

Chamberlain

An't please your grace, Sir Thomas Bullen's daughter--

The Viscount Rochford,--one of her highness' women.

KING HENRY VIII

By heaven, she is a dainty one. Sweetheart,

I were unmannerly, to take you out,

And not to kiss you.

The impression Shakespeare creates is that Henry had just set eyes on Anne for the first time, which is almost certainly untrue. Anne's popularity in the court, to say nothing of her being the sister of Henry's mistress and lady in waiting to Henry's queen, virtually guaranteed that he knew who she was, and he had probably noticed her attractions before. But the promiscuity of the French court was not openly tolerated in England; the king had but one mistress at a time, and just then his attention was taken up by Mary Boleyn.

Because Henry was discreet in his affairs, it is uncertain precisely when he began to pay court to Anne Boleyn, but it seems that they first became involved in 1525 and that their relationship remained secret until 1527. This was in spite of the fact that Anne was informally engaged to another man in 1523, Henry Percy, son of the Earl of Northumberland, one of the most ancient and prestigious titles in the English peerage. Their courtship was serious enough that they entered into a marriage pre-contract—meaning that Anne and Percy had only to consummate the relationship in order to be considered married in the eyes of the law, lack of ceremony or exchange of vows notwithstanding. Cardinal Wolsey, whose eyes and ears were everywhere in the English court, got wind of the contract, and he soon brought it to the attention of the King, without whose permission no aristocrat would marry without risking serious reprisals, up to imprisonment and loss of title and land.

King Henry was, naturally, annoyed that he had not been consulted, as he would have been in the case of any of his courtiers attempting to marry without his permission, but in this specific case, it seems that he had another motive for interference. As one historian puts it: "the thought of Anne Boleyn betrothed to another man disturbed [Henry VIII], so much so that he reluctantly confessed to the Cardinal the 'secret affection' he had been nurturing for her, and ordered Wolsey to break the engagement." Wolsey obediently upbraided Percy for involving himself with "that foolish girl yonder in the court, Anne Boleyn," explaining that, not only would Percy's father be certain to object, but the King had it in mind to arrange a match for Anne with another man. Neither Wolsey nor anyone else dropped the slightest hint that Henry was thinking of keeping Anne for himself. The Earl of Northumberland lost no time in marrying his son off to Lady Mary Talbot, and Cardinal Wolsey undertook the necessary legal measures to dissolve the pre-contract between Percy and Anne Boleyn.

Anne was understandably furious at this turn of events. She had no idea that the King was jealous of her relationship with another man, nor that he was in a fair way towards falling in love with her. She saw only that the unpopular, sinister Wolsey had seen fit to meddle in her affairs for no obvious reason. In fact, she was insulted, because Wolsey had told Percy that Anne was not a fit match for him. To add insult to injury, Anne was commanded to leave court and return to her father's estate for a year. On Henry VIII's part, this was a simple attempt to put distance between them, a distance that would hopefully quell his ardor for her. Anne saw it only as a banishment, a souring of her chances of making an illustrious and ambitious marriage, and she fumed her way through her exile until she was summoned back to court in 1525 and once again took up her place as one of the Queen's women. Throughout all of this, she blamed Wolsey, and determined to pay him back if the opportunity ever arose: "she would work the Cardinal as much displeasure as he had done her," she declared privately.

Anne was twenty-four by the time she returned to court in 1525. Queen Katherine was forty, and in the nadir of her disgrace. Henry was still closer in age to his wife than he was to Anne, but

Anne seemed to him the more fitting partner for his comparative youth and vigor. But before he had a chance to begin seducing his latest favorite, Anne began entertaining the advances of the poet Thomas Wyatt, who was married but whose wife was notorious for having extramarital affairs. Anne was too level-headed and ambitious to seriously consider compromising herself with a man who could not even marry her, but she permitted his attentions, taking them to be expressions of "courtly love", the fashionable style by which courtiers nourished a chaste devotion towards unattainable women, writing love songs and poetry in their honor. But the King grew jealous nonetheless. In the following year, 1526, it appears that Anne had finally figured out that Henry VIII was paying her pointed attention. She began to discourage Wyatt's attachment towards her, attempting to alter the terms of their relationship to those of mere friendship. This may have been merely to protect him, because evidence suggests that the King had made overtures towards Anne in private as early as 1525, and that she had rejected him—for good reason, as her sister Mary had been discarded without so much as a pension, let alone a title.

According to George Wyatt, Thomas Wyatt's grandson, Anne responded to Henry's initial overtures thus:

> "I think your Majesty speaks these words in mirth to prove me, but without any intent of degrading your princely self. To ease you of the labor of asking me any such question hereafter, I beseech your Highness most earnestly to desist, and to take this my answer in good part. I would rather lose my life than my honesty, which will be the greatest and best part of the dowry I shall have to bring my husband."

By "honesty", of course, Anne was referring to her virginity. That was the accepted mode for speaking of such things, which could not be referred to explicitly by high born women. To say that Henry was surprised by this response is probably an understatement. He could not have supposed her to be angling for marriage, not then; there was as yet no hint that he meant to have his marriage to Katherine annulled, and though it is perhaps possible that Anne was paving the way for a relationship after Katherine eventually died, it is more likely that she was simply protecting herself from the fate that inevitably befell a King's discarded playthings.

Supposedly, Henry's response to Anne's refusal was to say, "Well Madam, I live in hope." At which point Anne began to positively upbraid him: "I understand not, most mighty King, how you should retain such hope! Your wife I cannot be, both in respect of mine own unworthiness, and also because you have a queen already. Your mistress I will not be...how could I injure a princess [meaning Katherine] of such great virtue?"

Whether Anne spoke these precise words or whether this dialogue was reconstructed by Wyatt's grandson is immaterial; whatever she did say to Henry must have been similar enough to produce the same effect. In any case, Henry confessed his dilemma to Wolsey, who advised him that, "Great princes, if they choose to play the lover, have means of softening hearts of steel." And play the lover Henry did: he showered Anne with expensive gifts, and the fact that Anne accepted them has been taken as evidence by historians that Henry had confided to her that he was thinking of casting Katherine off, which would create an opportunity for her to become Queen. This may perhaps have been the case even as early as 1526, or she may simply have felt that rejecting the gifts of a King was a dangerous thing to do. As she, and other women, were to learn to their cost, the King's affection towards women could be a dangerous thing. He continued to feel terrible jealousy towards Thomas Wyatt, frightened that Anne was secretly in love with him, and that this was the secret reason for her refusal to sleep with him.

At some point towards the latter end of 1526 or early 1527, it seems that Henry at last took Anne fully into his confidence, explaining to her that, in his eyes, his marriage to Katherine was invalid, and that he intended to seek a papal annulment. At this point, Henry seems to have considered the outcome of such a request to be a foregone conclusion, as though he hadn't the faintest notion that he was on the eve of provoking one of the greatest battles ever fought by a King of England outside a battlefield. During this time, it seems that he must have proposed to Anne. Some historians consider this to be Anne's doing—that she had "cleverly manipulated him" into feeling such a heat of desire for her that he would be willing to do anything to get her into bed, even shake the very bedrock of the monarchy. But a period of several months passed between Henry's proposal to Anne and Henry's approaching Wolsey with a plan to make the annulment a reality, mostly because Anne herself was reluctant to commit herself.

While Anne was contemplating Henry's proposal, forestalling the moment when she would have to give the King a decisive answer, Henry's jealousy of Thomas Wyatt grew to such an extent that he packed Wyatt off to Italy on a diplomatic mission. By this time, Wyatt was in no doubt whatsoever as to the reason for the King's grievances against him—namely, that he and the King were in love with the same woman. Wyatt wrote his most famous poem during this period, chronicling the slow process by which he had come to realize that Anne could never love him, and that he was forbidden from attempting to persuade her because a more powerful suitor had come along to supplant him:

Whoso list to hunt, I know where is an hind,

But as for me, hélas, I may no more.

The vain travail hath wearied me so sore,

I am of them that farthest cometh behind.

Yet may I by no means my wearied mind

Draw from the deer, but as she fleeth afore

Fainting I follow. I leave off therefore,

Sithens in a net I seek to hold the wind.

49

Who list her hunt, I put him out of doubt,

As well as I may spend his time in vain.

And graven with diamonds in letters plain

There is written, her fair neck round
about:

Noli me tangere, for Caesar's I am,

And wild for to hold, though I seem tame.

"Noli me tangere" is Latin for "touch me not".
The poem clearly identifies Anne as Henry's
property, though this is almost an afterthought,
since it is Anne herself who frustrates Wyatt's
attempts to win her. To him, she is as
unattainable as a burst of wind he tries to
capture in a net. Wyatt wrote other poems about
Anne, but he destroyed or altered the references
to her in most of them. Only this poem, in which
he clearly gives ground to the King's suit, was
permitted to survive.

Love letters

To our modern perspective, Henry's six
marriages eclipse anything else that took place

during the course of his reign. His marriages seem to us a series of lewd spectacles, prompted by the monstrous ego of a supremely powerful man who callously discarded and even murdered women once they ceased to be of use to him. But even though Henry's personality changed for the worse between the beginning of the annulment suit and Anne's death in 1536, it is important to understand that, in 1527, Henry truly believed that his marriage to Anne would be his last. It wasn't only that he was maddeningly in love with her—in his eyes, she was going to help him save England from a bloody fate and endless civil war by supplying him with a son. Secondly, Anne Boleyn is so often represented as an ambitious schemer who would do anything, even ruin the life of a Queen, to get what she wanted, that we lose sight of the fact that it was Anne who was being courted by a powerful, charismatic man, the King to whom she owed her allegiance, and that she was not nearly as in love with him (or with the idea of marrying him) as he was with her. Henry's letters to Anne reflect this disparity—the one and only period during their relationship in which Anne had the upper hand.

The love letters which Henry wrote to Anne during their courtship are interesting because history tends to lose sight of the passionate, vulnerable, insecure human beings who wear the crown, our lens focusing instead on their political personae. But out of all the many letters Henry produced in his lifetime, his early letters to Anne offer us some of the most intimate glimpses available into his heart and mind during a period of his life when those organs were rather more tender and susceptible than they would be after another few decades of wear and tear.

Most of these letters date from 1527—the year in which Henry is thought to have proposed to Anne.

"My mistress and my friend,

"I and my heart commit ourselves into your hands, beseeching you to hold us recommended to your good favour, and that your affection to us may not be by absence diminished. For great pity it were to increase our pain, seeing that absence makes enough of it, and indeed more than I could ever have thought; remembering us of a point in astronomy, that the longer the days are, the farther off is the sun, and yet, notwithstanding, the hotter; so it is with our love, for we by absence are far sundered, yet it nevertheless keeps its fervency, at the least on my part, holding in hope the like on yours. Ensuring you that for myself the annoy of absence doth already too much vex me; it is almost intolerable to me, were it not for the firm hope that I have of your ever during affection towards me. And sometimes, to put you in mind of this, and seeing that in person I cannot be in your presence, I send you my picture set in a bracelet. Wishing myself in their place, when it should please you. This by the hand of your loyal servant and friends, H.R."

Anne's letters to Henry did not survive after her death. The only reason we have Henry's letters is because they were stolen and conveyed to Rome, where they were preserved in the Vatican archives. Nonetheless, it is known that when she replied to the above letter, she sent Henry a jewel: "a solitary damsel in a boat tossed by a tempest." Henry's response was ardent:

"For so beautiful a gift, I thank you right cordially, chiefly for the good intent and too-humble submission vouchsafed by your kindness. To merit it would not a little perplex me, if I were not aided therein by your great benevolence and goodwill. The proofs of your affection are such that they constrain me ever truly to love, honour and serve you, praying that you will continue in this same firm and constant purpose, ensuring you, for my part, that I will the rather go beyond than make reciprocal, if loyalty of heart, the desire to do you pleasure, even with my whole heart root, may serve to advance it. Henceforth, my heart shall be dedicate to you alone, greatly desirous that my body could be as well, as God can bring it to pass if it pleaseth Him, Whom I entreat once each day for the accomplishment thereof, trusting that at length my prayer will be heard, wishing the time brief, and thinking it but long until we shall see each other again. Written with the hand of the secretary who in heart, body, and will is your loyal and most ensured servant."

This letter was signed with a device: "H. autre AB (enclose in a heart shape) ne cherche R." HR, stood for Henry Rex, or Henry the King. Translated, it means "Henry the King seeks no other than the heart of Anne Boleyn."

In his next letter, he betrays the insecurity of a lover who is not yet certain that his beloved's regard for him will stand the test of a long separation. He chides her for not writing to him so often as he would wish, and ends by querulously wondering if she prefers being a long distance away from him after all:

"To my mistress: Because the time seems to me very long since I have heard of your good health and of you, the great affection that I bear you had prevailed with me to send to you, to be the better ascertained of your health and pleasure, because since I parted with you I have been advised that the opinion in which I left you has now altogether changed, and that you will not come to court, neither with my lady your mother, nor yet any other way. I cannot enough marvel, seeing I am well assured I have never since that time committed fault; methinks it is but small recompense for the great love I bear you to keep me thus distanced from the person of that she which of all the world I most do esteem. And if you love me with such settled affection as I trust, I assure me that this sundering of our two persons should be to you some small vexation. Bethink you well, my mistress, that your absence doth not a little grieve me, trusting that by your will it should not be so; but if I knew in truth that of your will you desired it, I could do none other than lament me of my ill-fortune, abating by little and little my so great folly."

The messenger who delivered the above letter into Anne Boleyn's hand had also another message to deliver, one too dangerous to commit to pen and paper: Henry had taken the first steps towards having his marriage to Katherine annulled. Anne's reply, apparently, was full of hearty congratulations for his success in a matter that she knew to be close to his heart, but though she declared herself his faithful and loving subject, the content of her letter was apparently not romantic enough for Henry's tastes. In the next letter he wrote to Anne, he abandoned simile, metaphor, and pretense, and asked her, in a straightforward fashion:

"...with all my heart, you will expressly certify me of your whole mind concerning the love between us two... If it shall please you to do me the office of a true loyal mistress and friend, and to give yourself up, heart, body, and soul to me, who will be and have been your very loyal servant, I promise you that not only shall the name be given to you, but that also I will take you for my only mistress, rejecting from thought and affection all others save yourself, to serve you only...."

By demanding these promises and pledges from her, Henry was asking, not only that she commit herself to being his wife in the fullness of time, but that she consent to become his mistress in the time being—to acknowledge their relationship publicly, in short. Anne had to tread carefully. She had no intention of sleeping with the King, lest he lose all respect for her; she was wise to understand that Henry would never crown as Queen a woman who had consented to have sex with him outside of marriage. But she could no longer keep him at a distance either. She decided to return to court, where she found herself regarded by Henry's courtiers as the one person who had full influence over the King. Indeed, even in the early days of their marriage, not even Katherine had been able to sway Henry's opinions as Anne could during this period. The fact that Henry and Anne were not yet sleeping together was not public knowledge, nor did anyone know that Henry intended to make Anne his wife. So harmless a figure did Anne seem at first that even Katherine embraced her, saying that she thought better of her maid of honor for having captured Henry's esteem. At that point, Katherine naturally assumed that, eventually, Anne would go the same way as her sister, and be discarded and forgotten by the King. But even after Katherine found herself the woman discarded by Henry, she rarely spoke any ill of Anne Boleyn, or permitted others to speak ill of her in her presence.

The King's Great Matter

In seeking to annul his marriage to Katherine, Henry was forced to act with the greatest secrecy and circumspection. For the most part, all of the attributes which had made Katherine a desirable bride for Prince Arthur twenty years ago—her ancient and august royal lineage, her powerful family, her reputation for kindness, piety, and virtue—were still in her possession. No one, not even a king, could discard the daughter of Isabella of Castile like she was an ordinary woman. An insult against Katherine—and the annulment was the gravest insult imaginable to a woman in her position—would be interpreted as an insult to all of her exalted relations, include the King of Spain, the Holy Roman Emperor, and the Pope who had made her marriage to Henry possible. Henry was risking war, excommunication, and every undesirable political consequence imaginable by pursuing an annulment. It was therefore of the gravest importance that no one should catch wind of the enterprise before Henry had marshalled all of his resources. It is no exaggeration to say that the annulment suit was planned with as much care and forethought as any military campaign.

When, in the late spring of 1527, Anne finally gave Henry her solemn promise to marry him as soon as he was free to do so, the next person Henry took into their confidence was her father, Thomas Boleyn, now Viscount Rochford. The Viscount was delighted. He had married well, but came of common stock; the idea that his daughter should be Queen, and his grandson King, was an honor he had never dreamt of. The other person taken into Henry's confidence was Cardinal Wolsey, who took a different view of the matter. Anne had never forgotten that Wolsey humiliated her by writing her off as no fit bride for Henry Percy, and no sooner did she begin to come into her own at court than Wolsey's other enemies—and there were many—formed a faction around her, having Wolsey's ruin as their object. Wolsey's opinion of Anne had not improved over the years, but now that she was Henry's acknowledged mistress, he was forced to court her favor. Anne had not softened in her desire for revenge against Wolsey, but Henry believed Wolsey was the one man in England who could make the annulment suit a success, so she was forced to treat him with equal cordiality for the present.

Despite the fact that Henry proceeded with considerable caution in the annulment suit, he underestimated the gravity of the undertaking. He believed it would over in a matter of months, a year at most; in fact, it took six years, beginning in 1527 and ending in 1533.

On May 15, 1527, in Westminster, Cardinal Wolsey presided, as papal legate, over an ecclesiastical court, attended by many other bishops and experts in canon, or church law. Historian Alison Weir describes the proceedings:

"The King was summoned and asked to account 'to the tranquility of his conscience and the health of his soul, for having knowingly taken to wife his brother's widow.' He admitted the charge, confessed his doubt, and asked for judgment to be given upon his case. Thereafter, the court re-convened for two further sessions and debated the matter, yet on 31 May the commissioners announced that the case was so obscure and doubtful that they were not competent to judge it. The King then consulted his Privy Council, who agreed there was good cause for scruple, and advised him to apply to the Holy See in Rome for an annulment, the Pope being the only authority qualified to pronounce on the matter."

And so the proceedings dragged on, to Henry's cost. It had been his intention that Katherine should be kept in ignorance of the affair for as long as possible, but shortly after the first ecclesiastical court was convened, Katherine received intelligence from the Spanish ambassador, who had already written to inform Charles V of Spain what was happening. From that point forward, Katherine became fearful of her own shadow, conscious that Cardinal Wolsey was having her watched for any unguarded statement, any shadow of misconduct on her part that might be used against her. The feeling that she was surrounded by enemies in a foreign court could not have been new to her, and the old anxieties it provoked undoubtedly caused her dreadful suffering.

In May of 1527, an event took place which spread at least some anxiety to its rightful source. Francis, the Holy Roman Emperor, marched against the Papal States with his armies, an event known as the Sack of Rome; effectively, the Pope himself was now Francis's prisoner. In other words, the person to whom Henry would have to apply for an annulment was now in the power of Katherine's own nephew. Rumors abounded in the English court, and Henry began to see that he could no longer keep Katherine in the dark—

as he believed she still was. On June 22, 1527, Henry called on Katherine in her apartments. He informed her that he was "much troubled in his conscience" about the dubiously lawful conditions under which they had been married, and that he had decided to separate himself from her. Assuming that the meekness and submission which had always characterized her behavior towards him would work to his advantage now, he asked for her obedience and cooperation. She should choose a house, any house she liked so long as it was at some distance from court, and an establishment would be formed for her there. She would not be left to suffer in poverty, as had happened after the death of Prince Arthur. She would merely cease to be Queen of England.

Katherine was heartbroken. The King, alarmed by her copious weeping, and perhaps pricked in his conscience, quickly changed his tune. He told her that his conscience demanded that an inquiry be made, but that the ecclesiastical trial might turn out in their favor, and their marriage proceed as before. When these "assurances" failed to calm her, he promptly turned on his heel and fled. This had not been the outcome he had hoped for. He wanted very much for Katherine to be on his side—that is, to keep his secrets. He certainly did not wish, or even seem to foresee the possibility, that she would begin to gather her own support base and resist his plans with all her might. But that is precisely what she did. Henry might claim to be troubled in his conscience, but Katherine was not so troubled. She was less sophisticated than Henry, but she possessed a moral certitude that was precisely calculated to stiffen her backbone in such a case as this. There was no doubt in her mind that she was Henry's true and lawful wife, in the eyes of God and man, that her daughter, Princess Mary, was Henry's true and lawful heir, and that Henry's "great matter" was founded on sheer moral bankruptcy. Still, she could not see Henry as the villain of the piece; she blamed Anne Boleyn and Cardinal Wolsey for perverting his mind to serve their mutual ambition. As one historian states:

"Henry himself came to feel that Katherine was allowing her earthly pride in her rank to stand in the way of his moral scruples, but it was not so much this as the fact that her pride would never allow her for a minute to acknowledge that she had been, not his wife, but his harlot for eighteen years. That pride, the abiding love she bore him, and the deep conviction that right was on her side would enable her to stand firm in her resolution until the day she died. In every respect other than that which touched her conscience, Katherine was ready to obey her husband, but in the event her conscience was to prove every bit as formidable as Henry's. Both were strong-willed people, and beneath the Queen's apparent meekness there was a layer of steely determination. The battle once engaged, neither would give any quarter."

In 1528, Katherine told the Pope's representative:

"Neither the whole kingdom on one hand, nor any great punishment on the other, although she might be torn limb from limb, could compel her to alter her opinion; and if, after death, she should return to life, rather than change her opinion, she would prefer to die over again."

She refused Henry's suggestion that she retire to a house away from the court, and instead continued about her daily life as though nothing had happened. There were no scenes, and no outbursts; she proceeded in the hope that, as Henry continued to treat her with the respect and honor due to his Queen, he might be reminded of the love they had once shared, and be persuaded to forget the evil scheme that he had been tempted into. Meanwhile, Wolsey continued to surround her with his spies, who were charged with intercepting any message that Katherine might attempt to pass to Charles of Spain or Francis in Rome. The fact that information about Katherine's plight did manage to make it Spain was due to the faithful service of the Spanish ambassador, Mendoza, who took it upon himself to act as Katherine's friend when she had few others.

By 1528, all of Europe knew that Henry VIII was seeking to dissolve his marriage, though few knew that he intended to marry Anne Boleyn. The proliferation of rumors made Henry intensely nervous; Katherine enjoyed extraordinary public popularity, and this, together with her powerful connections outside of England, made Henry worry that she was capable of inciting demonstrations at home and wars abroad. Katherine's cause was a popular one amongst women in particular, who saw in Henry a mirror of all their own straying, brutal, neglectful husbands. Crowds crying "Victory over your enemies!" greeted Katherine when she ventured outside the palace. At court, Katherine had fewer supporters; no one doubted that the King would eventually have his way, and thus, few people were willing to risk his displeasure by taking up Katherine's doomed cause. There were some exceptions, notably Thomas More. He maintained the position that Henry's marriage was lawful, and at first Henry accepted this; later, More famously lost his head for refusing to assuage Henry's conscience. Other supporters of Katherine included Mary Tudor, Henry's own sister, who loathed Anne Boleyn, and like Katherine, blamed her for the whole affair.

It was one thing, in the eyes of his people and his peers in Europe, for Henry to seek to rid himself of a wife who could not give him an heir; his fellow heads of state, at least, understood that Henry had a duty to safeguard the future of his country. But it was assumed by everyone, including Cardinal Wolsey, that Henry intended to make a traditional marriage once Katherine was out of the picture—that is, a marriage to a foreign princess. By the summer of 1527, however, the cat was out of the bag. Once it became generally known that Henry intended to marry Anne Boleyn, a commoner and his mistress, known in France as the sister of a woman who had once shared her favors with the French king, the tide of public opinion turned against him—and more pointedly, against Anne, who was reviled everywhere as a whore and a witch who had used diabolical arts to ensnare the king.

Anne, and the other members of her faction, were in fact using their arts, not to ensnare the King into a marriage he passionately wanted, but to poison his mind against Cardinal Wolsey. Wolsey, still ignorant of the King's design to marry Anne Boleyn, had been dispatched to France, thinking that he had come to negotiate for a marriage between Henry and a French princess. Anne and her supporters took advantage of his absence to persuade Henry that Wolsey was secretly doing everything in his power to persuade the Pope not to grant the annulment. Wolsey, having realized by now that Anne hated him, knew that his "hope of Heaven" lay in securing the annulment for Henry, but he also knew that he was helping to place in a position of power the very people who most wanted to see him destroyed. Wolsey's position was made all the more delicate when he was forced to return to England in September of 1527, having failed to gain the French king's support.

Unbcknownst to Henry, the Holy Roman Emperor and the King of Spain were united against him virtually from the start. Charles, the Emperor, had long since ordered the Pope neither to consider the annulment nor to allow the ecclesiastical trial to take place anywhere outside his dominion. None of the churchmen involved, from the Pope down, wanted to take responsibility for pronouncing a verdict in the case. Pope Clement himself suggested that Wolsey "pronounce the divorce himself" and afterwards seek Papal confirmation of the verdict. This would not satisfy Henry, however; the Pope must authorize the dissolution of his marriage as well as his remarriage, otherwise the heir of his union with Anne Boleyn might be subject to claims of illegitimacy. Hoping to tempt the Pope into shaking off his terror of Charles V, Henry mounted a campaign against the Emperor to liberate the Papal States and reinstate the Pope as head of his own lands, thinking that Clement would be more amenable to allowing the nullity trial to proceed once he was again his own master.

Campeggio

The King's "Great Matter" began in earnest in 1528 when Pope Clement dispatched Cardinal Campeggio from Rome, armed with a bull of decretal—that is, an official statement from the Pope declaring that Campeggio had been given authority to pronounce a verdict regarding the validity of Henry's marriage to Katherine. It took Campeggio some time to reach England, because

he suffered from agonizing bouts of gout—
indeed, this was probably one of the reasons he
was chosen for the mission, since the Pope,
Wolsey, and and virtually every other
ecclesiastical authority involved in the case
cherished the hope that if they simply dragged
matters out for long enough, Henry's ardor for
Anne Boleyn would begin to wane, and he would
lose interest in the whole affair. It was, perhaps,
a natural assumption; the King had tired of all
his other mistresses, over time. But few people
knew, or believed, that Anne was not sleeping
with Henry, and thus they underestimated the
depth of Henry's infatuation with her, as well as
Anne's instinct for playing the long game.

Henry was relieved when Campeggio arrived,
because the decretal bull was what had been
lacking during the preliminary trial conducted by
Wolsey—without one, it scarcely mattered what
the English bishops and cardinals decided. But
he was immediately annoyed again when
Campeggio urged him to make peace with
Katherine and reconcile himself to being married
to her. Once it was obvious to Campeggio that "if
an angel was to descend from Heaven, he would
not be able to persuade [Henry] to the contrary",
he turned next to Katherine, hoping to convince
her to enter a convent and become a nun. There
was some precedent for this; if Katherine took

holy orders, these would override her marriage vows, and only a Papal decree would be needed to allow Henry to remarry, a decree that Clement was very willing to give. Katherine was well-known for her piety, and this solution would allow her to retreat honorably from the field of battle without undergoing any serious disgrace—and it would also allow Princess Mary to remain the King's legitimate daughter, a status she would have to give up if the nullity suit was successful. Henry was delighted by this solution, and urged Campeggio to put it to Katherine as quickly as possible. But Katherine refused. "Although she is very religious and extremely patient, she will not accede in the least," Campeggio reported, adding that "she intended to live and die in the estate of matrimony to which God had called her." Katherine's steadfastness raised her in Campeggio's esteem, but left him without a solution to his problem.

Henry now resorted to a campaign of outright bullying. While Campeggio continued to urge her to become a nun, Henry's Privy Council drafted a letter to Katherine, warning her that she was suspected of inciting rebellion and backing an unspecified (and wholly fictitious) plot to kill both Henry and Wolsey. It stated that she was "a fool to resist the King's will" and threatened to banish her from court and permanently separate her from her daughter. The ladies of her household were continually harassed by Wolsey's spies, trying to find out anything in Katherine's conduct that could be used against her. Through all this, Katherine, though emotionally devastated, continued to conduct herself with gravity and composure. She ceased taking part in the social life of the court and devoted more time to prayer and devotions. At around this time, Anne Boleyn was finally given an establishment of her own and permitted to discontinue her service as Katherine's maid of honor, a situation which must have been deeply uncomfortable to them both.

Henry was in a delicate position himself when it came to public perception. All along, he had maintained the pretense that he would be deeply sorrowful if the papal commission found that his marriage to Katherine was unlawful, and that only the stirrings of his conscience had motivated him to subject them both to the inquiry. Nothing would please him more, he insisted, than that their marriage should be validated by the ecclesiastical authorities. In November of 1528 he made a speech to an audience of judges and commoners at Bridewell, where he claimed that:

"If it be adjudged by the law of God that she [Katherine] is my lawful wife, there was never thing more pleasant nor more acceptable to me, for I assure you she is a woman of most gentleness, humility, and buxomness—she is without comparison. If I were to marry again if the marriage might be good I would surely chose her above all other women."

At court, of course, it was well known that Henry was rapidly tiring of the very sight of Katherine, but it was easy to conceal this hypocrisy from general knowledge. And while the speech did a great deal of good for Henry's personal reputation, it did nothing to make Anne Boleyn less hated—everyone who knew of Henry's preference for her, save those who had hitched their political destinies to her rising star, loathed her.

Katherine's speech to the legatine court

Katherine refused to acknowledge the validity of the court assembled by Henry to try her—she had appealed to Rome for judgment, and declared that she would abide by no other ruling. Nonetheless, in obedience to Henry as his wife, she appeared at the trial convened on June 21, 1529, accompanied by the lawyers and prelates she had chosen to defend her, again at Henry's order.

When the court officials commanded her to come forth and take her place at the bar to testify, however, Katherine departed from the formal proceedings. She walked directly to Henry, seated on his throne, knelt before him, and made a long, articulate, impassioned speech:

"Sir: I beseech you, for all the loves that hath been between us, and for the love of God, let me have justice and right. Take of me some pity and compassion, for I am a poor woman and a stranger born out of your dominion. I have here no assured friend, and much less indifferent counsel I flee to you as the head of justice within this realm.

"Alas, Sir, where have I offended you? Or what occasion have you of displeasure, that you intend to put me from you? I take God and all the world to witness that I have been to you a true, humble, and obedient wife, ever conformable to your will and pleasure. I have been pleased and contented with all things wherein you had delight and dalliance. I never grudged a word or countenance, or showed a spark of discontent I love all those whom ye loved only for your sake, whether I had cause or no, and whether they were my friends or enemies. This twenty years and more I have been your true wife, and by me ye have had divers children, though it hath pleased God to call them out of this world, which hath been no fault in me. And when ye had me at the first, I take God to be my judge, I was a true maid, without touch of man; and whether it be true or no, I put it to your conscience.

"If there be any just cause by the law that you can allege against me, either of dishonesty or any other impediment, to put me from you, I am well content to depart, to my shame and dishonor. If there be none, I must lowly beseech you, let me remain in my former estate and receive justice at your princely hands.

"The King your father was accounted in his day as a second Solomon for wisdom, and my father Ferdinand was esteemed one of the wisest kings that had ever reigned in Spain. It is not therefore to be doubted but that they gathered such wise counsel about them as was thought fit by their high discretions. Also, there were in those days as wise, as learned men, as there are at this present time in both realms, who thought then the marriage between you and me good and lawful.

"It is a wonder to hear what new inventions are invented against me, who never intended but honesty, that cause me to stand to the order and judgement of this new court, wherein you may do me much wrong, if you intend any cruelty. For ye may condemn me for lack of sufficient answer, having no indifferent counsel. Ye must understand that they cannot be indifferent counsellors which be your subjects, and taken out of your Council beforehand, and dare not, for your displeasure, disobey your will and intent.

"Therefore, most humbly do I require you, in the way of charity and for the love of God, to spare me the extremity of this court, until I may be advertised what way and order my friends in Spain will advise me to take. And if ye will not extend to me so much favor, your pleasure then be fulfilled, and to God I commit my cause."

Throughout Katherine's speech, Henry, reportedly, did not look at her once. When she had finished, she curtsied, rose, and left the room, ignoring Henry's order that she return. Henry then turned to the courtroom, reiterating that there was "no fault in Katherine moved me!", but reminding all present how all but one of their children had died within weeks or hours of their births. He declared his belief that this had been God's punishment for his incestuous marriage.

The case continued to be tried, without either of the principle witnesses in attendance, for another ten days or so. At the end, Campeggio declared that that court must recess, and the matter referred to the Pope in Rome; unbeknownst to any but Wolsey, he had been given secret instruction by Clement not to make use of the decretal bull he had brought with him to England. Henry was furious, knowing full well that it might now be years before a verdict was rendered. His patience was worn thin, and his advisors lamented that no other business, no other affair of state affecting the nation, could be attended to while the King was distracted by the trial.

Chapter Three: Anne Boleyn Queen of England

Thomas Cranmer

Henry was infuriated by the suggestion that he, the King of England, should go to Italy to attend a trial. His anger against the Pope and the Holy See was coming to boiling point. In the mean time, Anne Boleyn was making a study of banned "heretical" literature written by advocates for church reform. Unbeknownst to Henry or Anne, their mutual discontent with the Church of Rome was shortly to be dignified by an unexpected advocate in the form of Thomas Cranmer, a forty-year old Cambridge divine who, while discussing the King's problem with colleagues over dinner one evening, made an ingenious suggestion that was shortly to make its ways to the King's ears. In Cranmer's view, the persons best suited to judge the thorny Scriptural issue at the heart of the King's case were not experts in church law from Rome, but doctors of divinity from the English universities who specialized in the interpretation of Scripture, not the laws of the institutional Church.

As soon as Henry heard of this conversation, he summoned Cranmer to his residence at Greenwich and ordered him to stop all his other work and dedicate himself entirely to writing a treatise, justifying the opinion he had perhaps only carelessly expressed to friends over dinner. Cranmer was giving lodgings with Viscount Rochford, Anne's father, so his needs would be looked after and no distractions would take his attention from his work. Cranmer quickly made friends with Anne and her father Thomas, who appointed him the family chaplain.

From the moment that Henry began to envision placing his fate in the hands of the English universities rather than in Rome, English history began slowly listing down the course it would take for the next five hundred years. Henry's entire view of the world was beginning to change. He saw that England was a small island nation, geographically and politically distinct from the rest of Europe, and the Church that reigned universally over all Christian nations was notoriously corrupt. The Church of England did not necessarily need the Church of Rome; indeed, why should it? Wolsey's star was waning rapidly; he had already been stripped of the office of Chancellor of England, and he was in so much fear for his life that he had surrendered several extremely valuable properties to Henry to secure his good will. As Henry grew less reliant on the Cardinal who had, all during his youth, been the power behind his throne, he began to conceive of a new future for England, one in which he was his own master, both politically and spiritually.

Time was of the essence, not only because Henry's royal patience was wearing thin but because Anne Boleyn was losing faith. She had never been as much in love with him as Henry was with her, and Henry, on some level, had always been aware of this—it only heightened her charms, in his view. But as the annulment proceedings dragged on, Anne began to doubt that her marriage to Henry would ever take place. She was already an old maid by Tudor standards, a virgin in her late twenties, and she had sacrificed a great deal for Henry's promises—her youth, her chance to elevate her status by marrying and having children. All she had to show for years of waiting was a reputation across England as a slut and a whore, a pile of rich gifts from Henry that nonetheless did not translate to status and security, and no sons. Since a common woman's status depended as much on being the mother of sons as did that of the Queen of England, Anne had good reason to feel that she had given up much and gained virtually nothing by remaining faithful to Henry.

As Henry grew increasingly conscious of Anne's disenchantment, so grew his need to have the annulment carried out as swiftly as possible, without more delay. He was terrified of losing Anne—ironic, considering that he would have her beheaded within three years of their marriage.

By Christmas of 1529, Henry had absolutely made up his mind that even if the Pope decided against him, he would not abide by the ruling. He announced as much to Katherine, declaring that "he prized and valued the Church of Canterbury as much as the people across the sea did the Roman." Nevertheless, in February of 1530, Henry sent Cranmer and an embassy of learned doctors to Rome to attend the crowning of Charles V, with instruction to press his suit, and to emphasize that the annulment was necessary "for the discharge of his conscience and for the quietness of his realm." This embassy did not retrieve the desired results, and in April of that year Henry informed the French ambassador that he no longer considered himself beholden to the Pope's authority. Katherine, meanwhile, was writing incessantly to the Pope, begging for his intercession, but by this point, Clement was afraid to take any action at all—if he supported Henry, he would gravely insult much of Catholic Europe, and if he supported

Katherine, he might provoke Henry to renounce Rome entirely.

One historian appraises Henry's state of mind during this period thus:

"After three years of tortuous negotiations to end his marriage, Henry was still obsessed with [Anne], and more than ever convinced that God was guiding his actions. He described his flexible conscience as 'the highest and most supreme court for judgement and justice', and...told the Queen he 'kept [Anne] in his company only to learn her character, as he had made up his mind to marry her. And marry her he would, whatever the Pope might say.' He was, in truth, no longer the same man who had lodged a plea in...ecclesiastical court in 1527. The despot was emerging, determined to have his own way, and even if necessary alter the process of law to get it."

The Death of Cardinal Wolsey

As egocentric and myopic as Henry's behavior might have been, the Pope's behavior was not much better, and it is scarcely surprising that Henry was losing faith in Clement's spiritual authority as the vicar of Christ on earth—he was, like so many Popes of that era, more a politician than a priest, lacking enough courage in his convictions to command anyone's respect. This became clear when he suggested that he might permit Henry to emulate Old Testament example and take Anne as his second wife, as an alternative to the annulment. Meanwhile, the man who had long been Henry's chief churchman, Cardinal Wolsey, was nearing the end of his career in Henry's service and on earth. Convinced by the Boleyn faction at court that Wolsey had been working against him in secret from the beginning, Henry had Wolsey arrested in November of 1530 on treason charges. Wolsey, however, was already in poor health, and died of illness whilst being transported to the Tower of London. As he lay dying, he was heard to remark, "If I had served God as diligently as I have done the King he would not have given me over in my grey hairs."

With Wolsey out of the way, Anne now began to give herself airs at court as though she were Queen already. "She is becoming more arrogant every day," remarked one observer, "using words in authority towards the King of which he has several times complained to the Duke of Norfolk, saying that she was not like the Queen who had never in her life used ill words to him." At one time, Anne had been as careful as Henry to pay Katherine all the outward forms and courtesies of respect due to her rank, but now she insulted her openly. The same observer noted, "That Lady Anne is braver than a lion...She said to one of the Queen's ladies that she wished all Spaniards were in the sea. The lady told her such language was disrespectful to her mistress. She said she cared nothing for the Queen, and would rather see her hang than acknowledge her as her mistress." That Anne Boleyn was very unlike Katherine of Aragon should have been apparent to Henry from the beginning, but the failure of their forthcoming marriage was virtually predicated on the fact that he expected Anne, once she was his wife, to conform to Katherine's image. Lack of sons and enduring sexual allure notwithstanding, Katherine was the Queen most ideally suited to Henry's temperament. He would not see her likeness again, save briefly in Jane Seymour, his third queen, and in Katherine Parr, the queen who outlived him.

King of England and Supreme Head of the Church

On January 5, 1531, Pope Clement finally and absolutely forbade Henry VIII, King of England, from marrying again if he should abandon his wife Katherine. A month later, on February 7, a Convocation of the clergy of York and Canterbury, the chief cathedrals in England, met to declare Henry VIII "sole protector and supreme head" of the Church of England, shortly after Henry stood before Parliament and demanded that the lords of the land recognize him as such. It was an historic moment: not only was the path being made clear for Henry to marry Anne Boleyn, but the English Reformation, which would lead both to a kind of Renaissance in that country and a veritable fountain of bloodshed for the next fifty years, was also ignited by this act. "From henceforth," writes Alison Weir, "the English Church would not recognize the Pope, who would be referred to as the Bishop of Rome, and he would not receive allegiance from the English bishops or enjoy any canonical jurisdiction in England." The repercussions would shake Europe to its foundations.

For the present, this was more of a political than a doctrinal revolution. The English church was Roman Catholic in all but name; it maintained all the traditional forms of worship and did not throw in its lot with Lutheranism, the only other recognized alternative to Roman Christianity in Europe. Religious practice in England would grow increasingly disunited during the remainder of Henry's reign, and during the brief reign of his son Edward. His daughter Mary, perpetually faithful to the memory and example of her faithful Catholic mother, would launch the Counter-reformation when she came to the throne, an attempt to bring England back into the fold of the Mother Church that would fail after her own early death. The Church of England would not begin to forge its own unique identity until the reign of her sister Elizabeth, who would usher in the use of a common prayer book, written for the English church by English divines. The Church of England would take an even more pronounced step away from Rome under the reign of Elizabeth's successor James, when the Authorized or King James translation of the Bible in English made the word of God accessible to anyone who could read.

By the early 17th century, the Church of England had acknowledged its doctrinal ties to Lutheranism, and Protestant Christianity had become an entrenched force in Europe, with strongholds in England, the German states, the Netherlands, and Scandinavia. For the first time, religious compatibility would have to be taken into account when arranging marriages between the royal houses of Christian nations. The German states were especially useful in this regard, producing a bevy of minor princesses whose small dowries were compensated by royal blood and a certain flexibility when it came to matters of religion: to bring about a sufficiently illustrious match for their daughters, German families were often willing that they should convert from the faith in which they were brought up to become Roman Catholics, or even Russian Orthodox.

But to speak of this is to speak of the far future. At the moment of Henry's confirmation, the people of England were more or less sanguine in their acceptance of the fact that he was "now effectively King and Pope in his own realm, with complete jurisdiction over his subjects' material and spiritual welfare." Anne Boleyn and her allies were, of course, more than sanguine; they were ecstatic. Only a few principled persons withheld their congratulations and approbations, including Thomas More, who now held the office of Lord Chancellor. A consummate politician, More attempted to walk a fine line between serving Henry's interests loyally, and obeying the dictates of his conscience, which could not countenance the break with Rome or the fate for which Katherine was now destined. For a time,

Henry was content for More to cherish his scruples privately, but as the dictatorial streak in his character became more pronounced, so his tolerance for any dissension would evaporate.

Despite the religious revolution which had just occurred, Henry still saw no easy path to getting rid of Katherine. He continued to badger her about taking holy orders and entering a convent. When she would not budge on this point, he tried to force her to desert him, by making her life at court difficult, but making it plain that if she took up residence elsewhere, he would consider this legal grounds for divorce. This was especially painful to Katherine because it prevented her from visiting Princess Mary, now fifteen, who was beginning to suffer from the bouts of continual illness that would plague her all her life. It grieved Katherine not to be with her daughter during her sickness, but she was fearful that if Anne Boleyn were to replace her, any children she bore Henry would threaten Mary's place in the succession. To protect her daughter's rights, it was necessary for Katherine to cling to her position as Queen for as long as possible.

Henry deserts Katherine

On July 14, 1531, Henry's court was due to relocate from Windsor Castle to Woodstock for the summer. When Katherine awoke early that morning, she and Princess Mary found themselves alone in the castle, with only their attendants. Henry had departed in the night without giving the Queen's household notice. A messenger reached her later in the day, informing her that Henry expected her to be out of the castle within the month. She could not have then been aware of it, but Katherine would never see Henry again. She sent word back to Henry by the messenger, saying that she was saddened that she had no chance to say goodbye to him: "Go where I may, I remain his wife, and for him I will pray," she said.

Henry, who had kept up a pretense of affection and respect towards Katherine since the beginning of the annulment affair in 1527, lost all remaining patience when he received this message, and exploded in anger. "Tell the Queen I do not want any of her goodbyes, and have no wish to afford her consolation!" he shouted at the messenger. "I do not care whether she asks after my health or not. Let her stop it and mind her own business. I want no more of her messages!" Katherine remained at Windsor until August, at which point Henry ordered her to leave immediately. For a time, she was given the use of a splendid house and continued to live as a Queen in all things, save that the King denied that she was his wife. Eventually, Henry would cease to support her in royal style; her continued defiance of his wishes had roused a streak of meanness and cruelty in his nature, and she would suffer for it to the end of her life.

On January 1, 1532, Henry installed Anne Boleyn in Katherine's former apartments and appointed her a lavish household of waiting gentlewomen. He spared no expense providing Anne with a wardrobe befitting a Queen. Yet even as the day approached in which she would be Queen in truth, she was losing the power base that supported her at court through the last five years. After Katherine was forced to leave Windsor, a mob of about eight thousand enraged Englishwomen marched on Anne Boleyn's house—their purpose was not clear, but it is quite possible they meant to lynch her or trap her in the house and burn it down around her. Anne escaped, but people throughout England continued to speak of her as a whore, an adulteress, a heretic, and a witch.

Moreover, Anne had managed to alienate some of her most staunch supporters amongst the nobility. This is one of the more baffling aspects of Anne Boleyn's character, and perhaps the most important to understand, as it speaks directly to her downfall in 1536. She was intelligent and well-read, and did not lack understanding of human nature, as her deft handling of Henry over the years proves. But she had a myopic streak; it was as if she lost all sight of the vulnerability of her position once she was assured that Henry was willing to move heaven, earth, and Rome for her sake. Perhaps she believed that, because the King himself was her devoted servant, it did not matter what anyone else thought of her. Granted, she had little control over what the people of England thought of her. Even if she had been more circumspect, it is unlikely that she could ever have been popular, considering that she was usurping the rightful place of a much-beloved Queen. But she need not, for instance, have alienated the Dukes of Norfolk or Suffolk, or Sir Henry Guildford, the King's comptroller, who elicited Anne's rage merely by speaking well of Katherine.

Though Anne was cleverer and more intellectual than Katherine in some respects, Katherine possessed an incalculable advantage over her: she was born royal, while Anne was born to a family of wealthy upstarts. Katherine, growing up surrounded by kings, queens, and courtiers, had consciously and unconsciously internalized valuable lessons which made her, arguably, a more effective politician than Anne could ever be. For instance, although Katherine probably never thought of it in these terms, by making herself well-beloved amongst commoners, servants, and courtiers alike, she was passively forming a faction that would support her in times of trouble, instilling such loyalty that they would brave the King's displeasure to support her. The fact that she was able to hold out against Henry's wishes for so long proves how powerful she had made herself simply by being generous, patient, and kind. It was a power that did not stem from the King, though he was considered the only source of power and privilege in the world of the royal court, and Henry seems to have been blind to its reach until it began to get in his way.

Anne, by comparison, shared Henry's view that all power stemmed from him, and she was so confident in her power over Henry that it seems never to have occurred to her that she might one day lose the ability to influence him. This was fatal naïveté on her part, but she had lived in a bubble for a long time—isolated from general society, living either with her own family or in Henry's court, wasting her youth and her best childbearing years, never certain whether Henry would be able to deliver on his promise. Anyone would be impatient, even irritable, under such circumstances, and since Anne's only consolation was the influence she enjoyed through Henry, perhaps she felt that the only outlet she possessed for her frustration and insecurity was playing the dictator to those closest to her. When Anne and Henry quarreled—and they did so frequently as the years wore on—it was usually Henry, not Anne, who quit the scene in tears. Henry was both the source of all her hope and all her frustration, so it is not surprising that she felt the need to lash out at him sometimes. But she would only be able to get away with this for as long as she had the upper hand in their relationship—that is, until she and Henry were married. Once she had taken Henry for her lord and husband, the balance of power reversed dramatically. But Anne did not seem to recognize this fact, and this formed the chink in her armor that left her vulnerable to the schemes of opposing factions in the court. Katherine, who had studied the nature of kings and sovereign queens all her life, would have known better, and could probably have given her useful advice. But Anne would never have taken it.

Still, regardless of how intemperate or unwise Anne's action may sometimes have been, in one sense—to Anne, perhaps the most important sense—she was successful beyond her wildest dreams, though she would not live long enough to know it. It was not chiefly love of Henry or even the wish to be Queen that motivated her, as she confessed to one of her maids of honor in 1532. She was determined to marry Henry, no matter how much she was hated for it, "that my issue may be royal, whatever will become of me." Anne probably died thinking that she had failed in this grandest of all schemes, since her only living child was a daughter, and she was declared a bastard after Anne's execution. But that daughter would, in 25 years' time, grow up to become one of the greatest and most famous monarchs in English history.

The marriage of Anne Boleyn and Henry VIII

On August 22, 1532, Archbishop Warham, of the See of Canterbury, died of old age and illness. Under the new organization of the Church of England, the Archbishop of Canterbury was second only to the King in authority. Warham had supported Henry in the separation from Rome, but he would not countenance his annulment from Katherine. Henry had tolerated his views, knowing that he was not long for the world. As soon as Warham died, Henry replaced him with Thomas Cranmer, the man who had shown Henry the way out of his difficulties with the Pope. Though Warham would never have countenanced Henry's marriage to Anne, Cranmer would do so enthusiastically; he had grown close to Anne and her whole family after Henry sent Cranmer to live with them. Furthermore, he believed that, as Queen, Anne would be a great patroness of church reform, a cause dear to his heart.

In September of 1532, Henry made Anne Boleyn a peer of the realm in her own right, an honor never before granted to a woman in England. She was named Marquess of Pembroke (Marquess is the male style, Marchioness the female equivalent). When she died, she had been stripped of her titles as Queen, and it was as Lady Marquess of Pembroke that she was condemned and beheaded. The conferral of Anne's peerage is interesting chiefly because of what it implies—namely, that after refusing to consummate a sexual relationship with Henry for five years, she had at last agreed to share his bed, probably after Archbishop Warham died. His death was the final true obstacle to her marriage to Henry, and she probably felt that it was safe at last to give him what he wanted.

Since there was now a possibility that Anne would become pregnant by Henry before they could be married—if Henry died in a sudden accident, for example—conferring a peerage on her was Henry's way of providing for her, and their child, in the event she never became Queen. The strongest evidence for the granting of the peerage being connected to Anne and Henry's sleeping together lay in the unusual haste with which the ceremony was organized and the pointed omission of some traditional language in the letters patent—normally, hereditary peerages can only be passed to legitimate children, but the word "legitimate" was excluded in this case. It seems likely that Henry was looking out for the possibility that Anne might bear his bastard.

By January of 1533, Anne knew herself to be indeed pregnant, and this prompted Henry to arrange the marriage ceremony with the greatest haste—and, at first, the greatest secrecy. Alison Weir describes the ceremony:

"Just before dawn, on the morning of 25 January 1533, a small group of people gathered in the King's private chapel in Whitehall Palace for the secret wedding of the King to Anne Boleyn. The officiating priest was either Dr Rowland Lee, one of the royal chaplains, or...Dr

George Brown, Prior of the Austin Friars in London and later Archbishop of Dublin. As Lee was preferred to the bishopric of Coventry and Lichfield in 1534, he seems to have been the likelier choice. There were four, possibly five, witnesses, all sworn to secrecy: Henry Norris and Thomas Heneage of the King's privy chamber, and Anne Savage and Lady Berkeley, who attended Anne. William Brereton, a groom of the chamber, may also have been present. Thus, in a hushed ceremony quite unlike the one she had hoped for, Anne Boleyn became Henry VIII's second wife."

The need for secrecy lay in the fact that, although Henry considered himself single and free to marry on the basis that his marriage to Katherine was not lawful, she was still legally his wife and he had not yet succeeded in officially nullifying their union. He had been holding out some hope for a papal decree in his favor, even offering to reunite the Church of England with the Church of Rome if Clement ruled for him. But with Anne pregnant, Henry could delay no longer. On his own authority, he declared his marriage to Katherine annulled, announcing to his Privy Council on April 7 that he was married to Anne Boleyn and that she was now pregnant with the child who would be heir to the English throne. Katherine was informed immediately afterwards by the Dukes of Suffolk and Norfolk, who traveled to her house at Ampthill (she had been forced to move several times since Henry abandoned her at Windsor, and each move brought her to a smaller house than the last) to tell her that she must no longer style herself Queen of England or attempt to communicate with the King. Henceforth, she would be known as the Dowager Princess of Wales, the style she was entitled to as the widow of Prince Arthur. Henry would no longer pay her an allowance, though she was permitted to keep her property. Katherine took the news calmly, but afterwards declared that she would use the title of Queen of England until she died.

Katherine was not the only one who took the news of the marriage in a rebellious spirit. Royal courts across the continent were scandalized; Katherine's nephew Charles V considered launching an invasion of England to restore her rights. There were public protests across England. When Henry ordered the English church to pray for Anne as their new Queen, the worshipers of one church in London walked out en masse. Nonetheless, on May 23, 1533, Thomas Cranmer, Archbishop of Canterbury, formally decreed that Henry VIII's marriage to Katherine of Aragon was "null and absolutely void...contrary to divine law". Five days later, he pronounced a second ruling: despite the strange circumstances, Henry's marriage to Anne was "good and valid" and the issue of their union would be "indisputably legitimate". Anne appeared before the public in a great procession, wearing ermine, on May 31, "and behind her streamed a great procession of courtiers and ladies, said to have extended for half a mile, and over her head the Barons of the Cinque Ports held aloft a canopy of cloth of gold with gilded staves and silver bells." Her coronation as Queen of England took place the following day, June 1, at Westminster Abbey.

Chapter Four: The Death of Anne Boleyn and the Wedding of Jane Seymour (1536-1537)

Foretelling doom

By the autumn of 1533, Katherine, still refusing to surrender her claim to the title of Queen of England, was removed at Henry's order to a small, damp, uncomfortable medieval castle at Buckden, where her allowance was reduced to a pittance. She would never see her daughter Mary again, for Mary had refused to acknowledge Anne as Queen, despite Henry's orders and Anne's repeated overtures. The last years of Katherine's life, she lived not unlike a nun, stretching her meager income as far as it would go so that she had money to spare for beggars in the neighborhood. She suffered much, but she did so with charity, courage, and a compassion that spoke of deep wisdom bordering on foresight. When her attendant spoke harshly of Anne Boleyn, Katherine "bade her hold her peace and 'pray for her', for the time would come when 'you shall pity and lament her case'." Katherine, after all, had known Henry since he was ten years old; probably no one still living knew him better than she. If anyone could have predicted

Anne's eventual fall from grace, it was probably Katherine.

It was an age of prophecies. The Nun of Kent had for years been prophesying that Anne would come to a bad end; she had such a popular following among Katherine's supporters that Anne ordered spies to watch her. And in May of 1533, when Anne's pregnancy had become visible, all the churches of England were commanded to pray for the safe delivery of a prince. But one William Glover, who had a reputation for correctly predicting the future, told Anne to her face that she would bear "a woman child and a prince of the land." No one was pleased by this prophecy at the time, but in light of later events, it makes one wonder where Glover was getting his information from.

Though Henry and Anne's marriage was only five months old, it was already beginning to show signs of strain. Anne's pregnancy made her either less sexually desirable or less sexually receptive to Henry, who decided to indulge in a brief affair with an unknown lady of the court. Anne reacted just as Katherine had reacted the first time she discovered Henry's infidelity, but unlike Katherine, she did not resign herself to meek forbearance once the first fit of anger was past. This came as something of a shock to Henry, who genuinely believed, despite all evidence, that the formalizing of their relationship would transform Anne into the sort of submissive wife Katherine had been. His knowledge of human nature, usually so keen, fell something short when it came to the women in his life. As to Anne's understanding of Henry, it was probably enlarged when he told her that, when it came to his infidelities, she must "endure as more worthy persons [had done]. She ought to know that it was in his power to humble her again in a moment, more than he had exalted her before." It is a chilling statement in light of Anne's eventual fate, and one can only wonder whether Anne was beginning to wonder if she got something more than she bargained for in Henry.

Princess Elizabeth

On September 7, 1533, Anne gave birth to her first and only surviving child, Princess Elizabeth. The birth of the future conqueror of the Spanish Armada and founder of English colonization in the New World naturally came as a disappointment to both of her parents. Henry had paid a number of astrologers and fortunetellers to predict the sex of his first child by Anne, and all of them had assured him that he was shortly to be the father of a son. But as had been the case with Katherine, Henry showed a capacity to be kind to his wife in the immediate aftermath of childbirth; he mastered his disappointment before he came to visit Anne, and when she apologized to him for the child's sex, and Henry merely remarked that they were both young and there would be time for sons later. Perhaps the reason he was so sanguine was because he was simply relieved that Anne had survived the birth—many women did not, especially women giving birth for the first time in their late twenties and early thirties. One wonders whether Henry knew that his mother, Elizabeth of York, had comforted his father, Henry VII, with almost the exact same words— "We are both still young enough"—after they received news of the death of his brother, Prince Arthur.

The infant princess was named for her two grandmothers, Elizabeth of York and Elizabeth Howard. In Shakespeare's play *Henry VIII,* Elizabeth's birth is the moment of redemption which makes good all the evil that have been suffered by Henry, whom Shakespeare depicts as the unwitting pawn of the villainous Wolsey, whose schemes deceive Henry into abandoning the deserving Queen Katherine. Shakespeare, writing a few years after the death of Queen Elizabeth, portrays a moment in which the good Thomas Cranmer, Archbishop of Canterbury, beholds the newborn princess for the first time and pronounces over her a speech which is part blessing, part divinely-inspired prophecy:

CRANMER

This royal infant--heaven still move about her!--

Though in her cradle, yet now promises

Upon this land a thousand thousand blessings,

Which time shall bring to ripeness: she shall be--

But few now living can behold that goodness--

A pattern to all princes living with her,

And all that shall succeed: Saba was never

More covetous of wisdom and fair virtue

Than this pure soul shall be: all princely graces,

That mould up such a mighty piece as this is,

With all the virtues that attend the good,

Shall still be doubled on her: truth shall nurse her,

Holy and heavenly thoughts still counsel her:

She shall be loved and fear'd: her own shall bless her;

Her foes shake like a field of beaten corn,

And hang their heads with sorrow: good grows with her:

In her days every man shall eat in safety,

Under his own vine, what he plants; and sing

The merry songs of peace to all his neighbours:

God shall be truly known; and those about her

From her shall read the perfect ways of honour,

And by those claim their greatness, not by blood.

Nor shall this peace sleep with her: but as when

The bird of wonder dies, the maiden phoenix,

Her ashes new create another heir,

As great in admiration as herself;

So shall she leave her blessedness to one,

When heaven shall call her from this cloud of darkness,

Who from the sacred ashes of her honour

Shall star-like rise, as great in fame as she was,

And so stand fix'd: peace, plenty, love, truth, terror,

That were the servants to this chosen infant,

Shall then be his, and like a vine grow to him:

Wherever the bright sun of heaven shall shine,

His honour and the greatness of his name

Shall be, and make new nations: he shall flourish,

And, like a mountain cedar, reach his branches

To all the plains about him: our children's children

Shall see this, and bless heaven.

KING HENRY VIII

Thou speakest wonders.

CRANMER

She shall be, to the happiness of England,

An aged princess; many days shall see her,

And yet no day without a deed to crown it.

Would I had known no more! but she must die,

She must, the saints must have her; yet a virgin,

A most unspotted lily shall she pass

To the ground, and all the world shall mourn her.

KING HENRY VIII

O lord archbishop,

Thou hast made me now a man! never, before

This happy child, did I get any thing...

Shakespeare's vision, needless to say, is flattering to both the princess and to her father. Henry's precise sentiments at Elizabeth's birth are not recorded, but they can be guessed at, based on the fact that he cancelled the week-long festivities which had been planned across the country to greet the birth of a prince. At least Henry was only a little disappointed; from the moment of her birth, the Princess Elizabeth's reputation was smeared with the same brush that vilified her mother. So many people regarded Henry and Anne's marriage as illegitimate that she was commonly referred to as "the little bastard". Even her older half-sister Mary greeted her birth with sneers. Anne, however, rapidly got over her disappointment at not having delivered a son; she loved Elizabeth passionately, keeping her by her side during court functions on a velvet cushions. She even wanted to breast-feed Elizabeth herself, though this was unheard of for highborn women, let alone Queens; Henry forced her to engage a wet nurse.

As with all royal children, Elizabeth was given her own house and establishment when she was still a baby—Hatfield Palace, where she would still be living when she received the news that she had become Queen at the age of 25. Meanwhile, her sister Mary's fortunes declined even as Elizabeth's star rose. She became known as the Lady Mary, not Princess Mary—a diminution in status which made it clear that despite being Henry's firstborn child, she was no longer her father's heir. She was sent to Hatfield to act as a maid of honor to her own sister, an insufferable humiliation which soured her relationship with Elizabeth for the rest of her life. Anne was interminably jealous of Mary, who still refused to acknowledge her rights as Queen, and threw a fit whenever Henry spoke of visiting to her or speaking with her. In Anne's eyes, any honor given to Mary was a threat to the status and privilege of her own daughter. During this period, Mary began to dream of leaving England, probably for Spain—but Katherine, though she was not allowed to see Mary, still wrote letters to her, and forbade her to think of abandoning her father, though he had effectively abandoned her.

The downfall of Anne Boleyn

When Henry had yet another extramarital affair during the period in which Anne was recovering from childbirth, the first rumors sprang up in the court that Henry was starting to tire of her. He had dismissed Katherine because she had not given him a son; he had been convinced that God would bless the dissolution of his unlawful marriage to his brother's widow by blessing his marriage to Anne with sons straightaway. When this did not happen, he seemed to find himself wondering why he had risked so much to be with her. Anne's extraordinary unpopularity with the people began to weigh on his conscience; it was a Queen's duty to be mother to her people as much as it was Henry's duty to be their spiritual and temporal father. Anne may have been the wife he desired, but even he could not pretend that she possessed Katherine's great gift—the common touch of a born Queen.

In July of 1534, Anne, in an advanced state of pregnancy, suddenly went into early labor, and the child was either stillborn or died shortly after birth. The event was not announced, nor was the sex of the child recorded, but it was probably a girl, since even a stillborn son would have gratified Henry in the knowledge that he was capable of fathering boys. Anne's grief and despair made her "very difficult to live with for a time." By this time, stress, repeated pregnancy, and disappointment had transformed Anne into a thin, tired-looking woman, and courtiers rejoiced to see that her influence over Henry was diminishing. He was taking lovers regularly, though he was discreet enough that their identities are not known; they were probably some of Anne's ladies, since the Queen's attendants were always chosen for their beauty and breeding, and this made them a tempting prospect to all the amorous gentlemen of the court. Anne began to realize that the failure of her second pregnancy had greatly diminished her worth in Henry's eyes. He began to speak of Anne as having been "corrupted" while in the French court; it is not certain what he meant by this, but Henry seems to have felt that she was not quite so virginal when she first came to their bed as she represented herself as being. It is possible that her sister, or other ladies who enjoyed dalliances with men at the French court, had simply passed sexual knowledge onto her, which Anne made use of, thinking it would please Henry.

By early 1535, observers at court noticed that Anne seemed stressed and anxious, as though she feared some great calamity. She felt that she was being spied on, and she probably was; having alienated so many of those who had supported her over the last five years, the anti-

Boleyn factions at court were now were more powerful than the pro-Boleyn factions. Alison Weir writes:

"It seems Henry had finally realized that marrying Anne had been a mistake. No longer did he see her through a lover's eyes: after two years of marriage, he was well able to regard her objectively, and could see little to impress him. Her arrogance, vanity and hauteur all proclaimed her inadequacy as a queen, and her public displays of emotion and temper were embarrassing. She had succeeded in making enemies of those who might have been her friends, and had displayed an unbecoming eagerness to wreak vengeance upon her enemies. She had probably lied about her virginity, and—worst of all—she had failed as yet to produce a son. Not only did Henry regret having married her, he had also brutally acquainted her with the fact. Yet, given any sign that he was contemplating her removal, the imperialists would be urging him to take Katherine back, something he could never contemplate. For the time being, therefore, Anne must remain; she might yet give him an heir. A son would still solve all her problems, as she well knew, but she told Henry early in 1535 that God had revealed to her in a dream that it would be impossible for her to conceive a child while Katherine and Mary lived. They were rebels and traitresses, she said, and deserved death. Henry failed to rise to her bait, another sign that her power was diminishing."

When Anne's third pregnancy ended in stillbirth in 1535, Thomas More, who was in prison awaiting execution for his refusal to sign the Act of Succession, made a prediction not unlike Katherine's, when she commanded her lady in waiting to pray for Anne, whose fate might soon become pitiable. More, like Katherine, understood Henry's temperament very well, and knew how quickly those whom he had held in great esteem could become the focus of his anger: "Alas, it pitieth me to remember into what misery, poor soul, [Anne] will shortly come. These dances of hers will prove such dances that she will spurn our heads off like footballs, but it will not be long ere her head will dance the like dance." When More was finally executed by beheading on July 6, his death sent shockwaves throughout Catholic Europe, and Henry's reputation as a tyrant was beginning to be assured. Henry himself wondered if he had gone too far this time, and, characteristically, he blamed Anne for bullying him into it.

Lady Jane Seymour

In 1535, Henry—no longer the slim, athletic, handsome youth he had once been, but an increasingly stout man of late middle age—began to take serious notice of the woman who would be his third queen and the mother of his only son. This was Lady Jane Seymour, daughter of Sir John and Lady Margaret Seymour, who had been sent to court as a young girl to act as Katherine's maid of honor, alongside Anne Boleyn. (Later she probably served Anne as well.) Jane was quiet and modest, taking Katherine as her role model for feminine grace and deportment, so she was not inclined to air her opinions publicly; still, she was known to support Katherine and Mary long after they were out of the King's favor. Jane was not as well-educated as Anne, or even Katherine, and she was less clever than either of them, but these were no detractions in the eyes of Tudor males. A woman who possessed less confidence in her own judgment was the more likely to submit graciously and be ruled by the wishes of her husband. Jane's chief talents were in needlework—she was famous for her embroidery—and she was fond of riding and hunting.

At 27, Jane was considered anything but a beauty—she was thought to be rather plain, in fact—but she presented a remarkable contrast to Anne at the very moment when Anne was least attractive to Henry. Jane had studied at Katherine's court how to emulate modest feminine virtues, and Henry had come to realize how much he preferred meek, submissive women to viragos like Anne. By 1535, Henry was attempting to entice Jane to become his mistress, but like Anne, she put him off, unwilling to surrender her virginity in an extramarital affair. For all Jane's modesty, however, there is no doubt that she was ambitious, even if she was not as inclined as Anne to risk everything to pursue that ambition. But the Seymour family, especially the men, were more than ambitious enough on her behalf to seize the opportunity that Henry's partiality for her presented. They had long loathed Anne Boleyn and all her supporters.

Before long, Henry was openly paying court to Jane just as he had done with Anne while Katherine was still his wife. If Jane was not as clever or learned as Anne, she had nonetheless studied the tactics Anne had used to win and keep Henry's affections. Jane, to her credit, had a different sort of ambition from Anne's—she wished to encourage Henry to reconcile with the

Pope, with his forsaken wife Katherine, and most of all with his daughter Mary. Both Mary and Katherine were very ill, Katherine in the last stages of the cancer that would kill her, and it had been years since Mary had spoken to her father. Jane wanted to be Queen, but she also wanted to use her position to do good and relieve the suffering in Henry's sundered family.

The death of Katherine of Aragon

For years, particularly since the birth of Princess Elizabeth, Anne Boleyn had wished for and plotted the deaths of both Katherine and Mary. She believed, mistakenly, that Katherine's very existence was a threat to her safety; in fact, now that she had lost Henry's love, it was only Katherine's life that stood between Anne and a grim fate, because Henry would not dare rid himself of his present wife while his former wife was still living.

Katherine had suffered intensely over the last several years, being forced to move from house to house, several of which were chosen on purpose because they were known to be unhealthy. Henry would not countenance killing

Katherine outright, but he hoped very much to hasten her end by exposing her to poor living conditions. In the end, however, it was not typhus or cholera or sweating sickness that killed Katherine, but cancer. On the last evening of her life, at the age of fifty, Katherine, aware that she could not live much longer, took pen to paper and wrote a letter of farewell to the man she still regarded as her husband:

"My lord and dear husband: I commend me unto you. The hour of my death draweth fast on, and my case being such, the tender love I owe you forceth me with a few words to put you in remembrance of the health and safeguard of your soul, which you ought to prefer before any consideration of the world or flesh whatsoever; for which you have cast me into many miseries, and yourself into many cares. For my part, I do pardon you all, yea, I do wish and dearly pray God that He will also pardon you. For the rest, I commend unto you Mary our daughter, beseeching you to be a good father unto her, as I have hitherto desired...Lastly, I vow that mine eyes desire you above all things."

She died at about 2 pm the next day, on January 7, 1535, after hearing a final mass and receiving extreme unction. She died a saint in the eyes of many, who had observed her long and patient sufferings, and the charity she rendered unto others until the end of her life. Katherine was buried in a lavish state funeral, where she was accorded the honors of the Dowager Princess of Wales; but in the early 20th century, Queen Mary of Teck, husband of King George V of England, ordered that "the symbols of queenship" were to adorn Katherine's grave. There they remain still—banners bearing the royal arms of both Spain and England.

Ironically, it was Henry who rejoiced when he learned of Katherine's death, and Anne who was troubled. With her rival gone, there was now no doubtful shadow over her right to be known as Queen of England. Yet she was aware that if her present pregnancy did not result in the birth of a healthy boy, Henry would have no reason not to treat her as he had done Katherine, or worse.

The Death of Anne Boleyn

Anne Boleyn was executed at 8 o'clock in the morning on May 19, 1536, beheaded by a specialist swordsman who, at her request, had been sent for from France to perform the task.

Beheadings were often brutal butcheries; it was not uncommon for less skilled headsmen to require two or three blows to successfully sever the head from the neck. Beheading was considered a more merciful death than burning at the stake, but when carried out by a clumsy executioner, a death that was intended to be painless could be agonizing.

Exhausted after two sleepless nights, dazed by the sunlight, Anne climbed the scaffold and asked that the executioner not strike her until she had made a short speech before the people. This permission was given, and she turned to face the crowd, speaking with courage and conviction:

"Good Christian people, I am come hither to die, according to law, and therefore I will speak nothing against it. I come here only to die, and thus to yield myself humbly to the will of the King, my lord. And if, in my life, I did ever offend the King's Grace, surely with my death I do now atone. I come hither to accuse no man, nor to speak anything of that whereof I am accused, as I know full well that aught I say in my defense doth not appertain to you. I pray and beseech you all, good friends, to pray for the life of the King, my sovereign lord and yours, who is one of the best princes on the face of the earth, who has always treated me so well that better could not be, wherefore I submit to death with good will, humbly asking pardon of all the world. If any person will meddle with my cause, I require them to judge the best. Thus I take my leave of the world, and of you, and I heartily desire you all to pray for me."

She then said goodbye to her ladies in waiting, giving them some personal tokens to remember her by, and prayed with a priest. Then the headsman asked her forgiveness, as was traditional; she gave it, allowed one of her ladies to blindfold her, and laid herself down on the block. All the people watching fell to their knees, out of respect. The expert headsman took her head off with a single stroke before displaying it to the crowd. The eyes and mouth continued to move for a few seconds before falling still.

How did Anne come to meet such a fate after her triumphal rise from minor noble to Queen of England? Everything we have already learned of her character, and Henry's, and the gradual disintegration of their relationship, accounts for it. The final blow arrived in the form of a miscarriage Anne suffered in early 1536; the fetus, only about 15 weeks old, looked as though it would have been male. Anne was disconsolate, understanding that her last hope of keeping Henry's favor was gone, and this time, Henry was not diplomatic when he came to visit her. He blamed her for "the loss of his boy"; Anne declared that the fault lay with him, because he had been unkind to her. Henry then declared that she "should have no more boys by him." The message was clear: Henry was finished with her. He never visited her bed again. In his mind, his marriage with Anne was over. All that remained was finding a pretext by which he could lawfully be rid of her, and this was easily found once he turned to his advisors for help. Henry declared to Eustace Chapuys, Charles V's ambassador to England and Katherine of Aragon's most faithful champion during her life time, that "he [Henry] had made this marriage seduced by [Anne's] witchcraft, and for that reason he considered it null and void, and that this was evident because God did not permit them to have male issue, and that he believed he might take another wife."

Even to Chapuys, who had long regarded Henry's treatment of Katherine with disgust, and was no admirer of Anne's, it was shocking to think that the king would divorce another wife, only three years after their marriage. But Henry was not contemplating divorce. After the protracted legal battle that had surrounded his efforts to rid himself of Katherine, he was determined that Anne should be excised from his life with dispatch. The fact that Henry had made a point of mentioning witchcraft to Chapuys would seem to indicate that he intended to have Anne killed from the first. Everyone in the early 16th century believed in the existence and the power of witchcraft—so much so that it was a capital offense, punishable by death. If Anne could be proven to have dabbled in witchcraft, she would be executed as a matter of course.

Anne's death was arranged swiftly because it suited the political ambitions of many people, not just the King. England was under boycott from certain Catholic nations who would no longer trade with a country whose king had nearly been excommunicated. And now that Katherine was dead, the Holy Roman Emperor was extremely anxious that measures be taken to safeguard the interests of his cousin, Lady Mary, and ensure her place in the line of succession. It was well known that Henry was in love with Jane Seymour and that he would probably marry her as soon as he was free. This was the best possible outcome to Charles V, because he knew that, as Queen, Jane would do her best for Mary. On Charles' instructions, therefore, Chapuys advised Jane to "drop heavy hints about Anne's heretical leanings in Henry's ear, and to say that the people of England would never accept her as their true Queen. She must say these things in the presence of her supporters, who would all then swear, on their allegiance to the King, that she spoke the truth." Apparently, Jane took Chapuys' advice, and the effect on Henry was predictable.

By February 1536, about a month after Anne's final miscarriage, Henry had finally made up his mind to marry Jane Seymour, and just as his falling in love with Anne had confirmed his resolution to annul his marriage to Katherine, his newfound passion for Jane sealed Anne's fate. Henry had sent Jane away from court, to keep Anne from abusing her, since Jane was still one of her ladies. Suffering the pangs of love during their separation, Henry sent a messenger to Jane's home with a "love-letter and a purse of gold". Jane's reaction to these gifts made a striking impression on Henry, and on his messenger:

"Until now, Jane had not scrupled to accept expensive gifts, but even she drew the line at accepting money. Instead...she kissed his letter with great reverence, then handed it back unopened to Sir Nicholas. Then, falling to her knees, she asked him to beg the King on her behalf to consider that she was a prudent gentlewoman of good and honorable family, a woman without reproach who had no greater treasure in this world than her honor, which she would not harm for a thousand deaths. If the King wished to send her a present of money, 'she prayed him to do so when God might send her a husband to marry'."

This was a calculated display of maidenly modesty that exceeded even Anne Boleyn's arts—probably because it was predicated on a deeper understanding of Henry's character. From this point forward, Henry was determined to marry Jane, and to prove the honor of his intentions, he declared that henceforward he would only speak to Jane in the presence of her own family. To facilitate this arrangement, he had Jane's brother Edward and his wife Anne installed in secret apartments that connected with the royal chambers, and ordered Jane to take up residence with them. That way, Henry could speak to her when he liked, with her brother and sister in law close by to chaperone the exchanges.

It was Thomas Cromwell, one of Henry's more sinister advisers, who struck on a means of implicating Anne in a treasonable offense. Cromwell informed Henry that his spies, who watched Anne continually, had given him good reason to believe that she was adulterous, resorting to sex with other men in her desperation to become pregnant. If she could be linked in an adulterous affair with a man against whom evidence might be found—or manufactured—proving that he had designs against the King's life, then Anne might be implicated in a murderous conspiracy. She could then be charged and convicted of high treason, and executed. Both Henry and Cromwell were certainly conscious, at least in their own minds, that they were manufacturing a scheme to kill an innocent woman—at least, a woman innocent of the crimes for which they intended to execute her. But Henry was King, surrounded by servants who wished to gain his favor by carrying out his will; he had only to hint and suggest in order for those servants to produce evidence to convince him of what he wanted to believe.

On May 2, 1536, Anne's one-time supporter and admirer, the Duke of Norfolk, arrived at her apartments with a contingent of other nobles, and declared that it was the King's pleasure that she be confined a prisoner in the Tower of London for the crime of adultery. She was informed that her partners in these adulterous acts had already confessed their guilt. Anne was calm at first; she knew that she was innocent of adultery. But along the journey, Norfolk taunted her, and by the time the barge arrived at the Tower, she was distraught. "I am the King's true wedded wife! Oh my mother, my mother!" she cried out in anguish. Then, regaining her composure, she said, "My God, bear witness there is no truth in these charges. I am as clear from the company of man as from sin." She was too clever not to understand what was happening to her. Queens convicted of adultery in the past were merely confined to nunneries, but this, clearly, was not to be her fate. The obvious falsehood of the charges laid against her pointed clearly to a conspiracy, organized by men who cared nothing for the truth, and were willing to do anything to be rid of her—as Henry had been willing to do almost anything to be rid of Katherine.

Seventeen days later, she was dead. All the preparations for her imprisonment and trial had been made in the greatest secrecy. Henry did not want to give Anne the chance to do as Katherine had done and apply for help from any allies she might possess abroad. Nor was he going to give her the opportunity to think her way out of the trap he had set for her. He had made certain that by the time Anne was arrested, the entire machinery of her condemnation and execution was already set in motion. It was cruel beyond imagining, but compared to the slow, protracted cruelty of his behavior towards Katherine, there is perhaps something to be said for the swiftness of its dispatch.

In her lifetime, Anne Boleyn had hounded Cardinal Wolsey to his death, done everything in her power to have Katherine and Mary killed, and probably poisoned at least one Privy Councilor who disliked her. She was not guilty of the charges she was condemned for, but Henry, remembering her conduct of the last nine years, found it all too easy to believe that she was vicious and morally bankrupt. By this point, it was an opinion shared by almost all who knew her, save her own family, and Archbishop Cranmer, who had admired her from the first. He was saddened when he learned what her fate was to be:

"My mind is clean amazed, for I never had better opinion of woman, but I think your Highness would not have gone so far if she had not been culpable. I love her not a little for the love which I judged her to bear towards God and the Gospel. Next unto your Grace, I was most bound unto her of all creatures living."

Later, on the day of execution, Cranmer encountered a colleague who confessed to him that he had suffered a terrible nightmare the night before in which he saw Queen Anne's head detached from her body. He was not aware of the fate that was shortly to befall her, but Cranmer told him. "Do you not know what is to happen today?" he said, looking sad. "She who has been the Queen of England on earth will today become a queen in Heaven."

Jane Seymour, Queen of England

Henry's betrothal to Jane Seymour was announced to his Privy Council immediately after the guns fired, signaling that Anne was dead. Jane herself was in her chambers, already preparing her wedding clothes. The enduring historical image of Jane Seymour is of a modest, virtuous woman, a passive servant to the wishes of the powerful men who surrounded her. As she was the only one of Henry's queens to die a natural death (at least, while still married to him), it was inevitable that she would be remembered as the best, most modest, and gentlest of all his wives. But she was not without ambition, or agency; she knew perfectly well that the further she advanced in the King's graces, the more likely Anne, who was her sworn mistress, was to come to a bad end. If her method of seducing Henry differed from Anne's, it did not necessarily mean she was more virtuous, only that she was more subtle.

Jane's image as a virtuous, retiring female was held in some doubt by courtiers who found it difficult to believe that a woman of Jane's age could be part of the English court for so long without having lost her virginity to some man or another. Chapuys, however, reflected that the King would not be angry if he married her and found she was not a virgin, "since he may marry her on condition she is a maid, and when he wants a divorce there will be plenty of witnesses ready to testify that she was not." What Chapuys left unsaid was that such witnesses would be easy to find whether or not the charge was true.

Alison Weir accounts for Henry's attraction to Jane Seymour by observing that, though she was rather plain, she was "Anne Boleyn's opposite in every way. Where Anne had been bold and fond of having her own way, Jane showed herself entirely subservient to Henry's will; where Anne had, in the King's view, been a wanton, Jane had shown herself to be inviolably chaste. And where Anne had been ruthless, he believed Jane to be naturally compassionate. He would in years to come remember her as the fairest, the most discreet, and the most meritorious of his wives."

On May 19, 1536, the day of Anne Boleyn's execution, Henry left the palace to stay at Hampton Court for a week. The next morning, Jane joined him there, and they were formally betrothed in the presence of Jane's family. They were married ten days later in a private ceremony on May 29th at Whitehall Palace. She was publicly proclaimed Queen of England on June 4th. For at least some members of Henry's court there must have been a sense of the surreal to the fact that Anne had so recently been presiding with Henry over banquets, entertainments, and other court functions, only for those functions to now fall to a different woman, without even a traditional period of mourning to separate the two regimes. Jane settled into her role quickly, choosing 200 young women to fill her retinue as maids of honor, and though she was a compassionate mistress, she soon proved herself a stickler for hierarchy, less tolerant of liberties than Anne had been. Nonetheless, she managed to maintain the formalities without appearing arrogant. One observer remarked that Queen Jane was, "as gentle a lady as ever I knew, and as fair a queen as any in Christendom. I do assure you, my lord, the King hath come out of hell into heaven for the gentleness in this, and the cursedness and the unhappiness in the other. When you write to the King again, tell him that you do rejoice that he is so well matched with so gracious a woman as she is."

Jane's goals as Queen were threefold: first and foremost, she wanted to remain in Henry's favor, thus avoiding the fates of her two predecessors. Her lesser goals included providing him with a male heir, advocating for the advancement of her Seymour relations, and healing the breech between Henry and his daughter Mary, now twenty years old, who remained estranged from him because she would not sign the articles that acknowledged Henry head of the Church of England, or confirm the invalidity of his marriage to her mother. Henry was so furious with Mary for what he perceived as her obstinacy that he had not seen or spoken with her for years—their only communication came in the form of delegations of nobles sent to her house to browbeat her into signing the Act of Succession. Shortly after Henry and Jane were married, Jane attempted to speak of bringing Mary to court, but Henry berated her for her interference; it was a sharp, early lesson that Henry was long past the days when he would do anything to please the woman he professed to love.

Mary was at last reconciled to her father when Chapuys, the Emperor's ambassador, conveyed to her the Pope's assurances that she would be pardoned in the eyes of God for signing the articles proclaiming her mother's marriage invalid, since she was being compelled to do so against her will. Only the most intense suffering, both physical, mental, and spiritual, could have compelled her to do it, and she regretted it for the rest of her life. Henry was placated and Queen Jane was delighted. In the Lady Mary—for she could no longer claim the title of Princess—Jane would have a companion of rank suitable to be her close companion. She was too sensible of the difference between her station and that of her maids and ladies to make friends and confidantes out of them, so naturally she felt rather lonely at court. Henry wrote to her, assuring that once she was well again—for Mary was nearly always sick—he would bring her to live at court with him. Jane, aware that Mary had been living in near poverty for years, undertook to provide Mary with a suitable wardrobe. Shortly afterwards, Henry declared to his ministers that Mary's place in the succession had been restored—she would be first to inherit the throne of England after any children born of his union with Queen Jane.

Having seen Henry reconciled with his daughter, Jane made only one other attempt to use her influence with him in a matter of politics. On the pretext of investigating church corruption, Henry began closing all the convents and monasteries in England, seizing their money and lands to replenish the national treasury. Jane, an orthodox and fervent Catholic, fell to her knees and begged Henry to, at least, preserve a few of the smaller abbeys and priories. Henry's anger was explosive, and he reminded Jane that "the last queen had died as a result of meddling too much in state affairs." Jane took the rebuke to heart; like Katherine, she believed that her first duty was to obey her husband. She never attempted to sway him in matters of policy again.

Family, birth, and death

Lady Mary was brought to Windsor for the Christmas festivities in 1536. Henry greeted her warmly, then presented her to his Queen, and Jane embraced her, calling her Henry's "chiefest jewel in England." Mary was so overcome by the enormous shift in her circumstances that she fainted, and had to be revived by her father. From that point until Jane's death, she was at court more often than not, and she and Jane became close friends. At this point, with Anne dead, Mary seems to have discovered her sisterly feeling for Elizabeth, was who then an extraordinarily precocious three-year old. It was through Mary's intercession that Elizabeth was brought to court, and though she was too small to spend too much time with the adults, Henry played with her often, and it was apparent to all who observed that he doted on her.

By the spring of 1537, it was also apparent that Queen Jane was pregnant, about three or four months along. Henry had decided long ago that their first son would be named Edward. The pregnancy was announced to the realm in April of that year, and by May, Jane was able to feel the child stirring. She lived retiringly during her pregnancy, though Henry spared no expense for her comfort, and when she began to have cravings for quail he ordered a shipment of them from France, as they were out of season in England.

Jane was due in October. In September, Jane moved to Hampton Court to be ready for the lying in, occupying the same chambers where Anne Boleyn had once awaited the end of her own pregnancies. In the last few weeks of her confinement, she was attended constantly by Lady Mary; Jane was in terror, because the plague was rampant in London, and she feared that it would spread to Hampton and infect her or the baby. Since crowding was known to facilitate the spread of the plague, Henry and his household moved to nearby Esher, so that fewer people would be crammed into the confines of Hampton Palace. It was the furthest from her he dare go, in case she needed him, "considering that, being a woman, upon some sudden and displeasant rumors that might by foolish or light persons be blown about in our absence, she might take to her stomach such impression as might engender no little danger or displeasure to that wherewith she is now pregnant, which God forbid."

Jane went into labor on October 9th, 1537, and the labor lasted for three days and nights. Obstetrical medicine was nonexistent at the time; births were attended by midwives, not doctors; nearly as many mothers and children died as lived. Jane's sufferings were undoubtedly immense, and in the end, complications from the delivery would kill her. But on October 12, 1537, she finally gave birth to a son, the future King Edward VI. He was said to look like Henry but have his mother's fair coloring, compared to his sister Elizabeth who looked like her mother but had Henry's red hair. He was healthy and without defect, and a messenger was sent to Henry posthaste. Unsurprisingly, the King was delirious with joy, and the entire country joined in his celebrations. Thanksgiving masses were sung throughout the nation and in London the bells pealed for a day and night, while guards at the Tower of London shot 2000 rounds of ammunition. People held impromptu street festivals, rather like potlucks, and churches offered feasts to their parishioners.

At first, it seemed that Jane was recovering from the birth as quickly as might be expected. Then, the day after Prince Edward's christening, four days after the birth, she became suddenly ill. Within a day or so she was so weak that it was believed she was on the verge of death. Just before last rites were about to be administered, however, she seemed to regain her strength. This reprieve did not last long, however; soon she was delirious with fever. Henry rushed to her bedside at eight in the evening on October 23rd; by the evening, she was unconscious, and she died at two in the morning on October 24th. The cause of her death was undoubtedly puerperal fever, an infection resulting from a tear in the perineum during the birth which became infected, then septic. It was one of the chief killers of women before the discovery of microbe theory and antiseptic hygiene practice.

Henry could not bear to remain in the same house as Jane's dead body; all his life, he had felt an almost childlike horror of anything to do with illness and death. For several days he remained secluded in his apartments at Westminster, charging the Duke of Norfolk to oversee the funeral preparations. Lady Mary, who probably mourned the Queen's death more than any other person save for her immediate family, was the chief mourner at the ceremony. When Henry emerged from his seclusion a few days later, he was met by a delegation of advisors who, somewhat tentatively, suggested that he consider marrying again. True, England now had a male heir; but the prince was a newborn, and infants died suddenly almost more often than not. To the ministers' relief, they found Henry amenable to their suggestion. "He has framed his mind to be indifferent to the thing," one of his councilors remarked.

Six years later, near the end of Henry's life, he commissioned a group portrait of himself, his three children, and his Queen—not the one he was then married to, Katherine Parr. "For Jane," writes one historian, "this represents a considerable achievement, considering that her career, from her meetings with the King at Wulfhall in the autumn of 1535 to her death at the height of her triumph in 1537, had lasted just two short years." When Henry VIII died in 1547, he was buried with Jane.

Chapter Five: Anne of Cleves (1540)

Henry as bridegroom (again)

By 1540, Henry had been without a wife for two years and two months. This has been interpreted as a compliment to Jane's memory, but in fact, he had begun courting foreign princesses soon after she was laid to rest. For over a year, he had been unsuccessful, but in 1540, after a year of negotiations, he found himself engaged yet again.

Had he not been King of England, one wonders whether Henry would have been able to persuade another three women to marry him. He was no longer the dashing, athletic, handsome prince of former days. During his marriage to Anne, a venous ulcer had developed on his leg— it became a suppurating open wound that smelled bad and would not heal or close, not matter what his doctors did for him. The pain of the wound meant that he was unable to take as much exercise as he used to, and now, at the age of 48, he had run to fat. The pain he suffered— not merely from the wound, but from the migraines which had afflicted him since he was young—made him irascible, prone to temperamental outbursts. When he became King of England at the age of 18, he was considered not only charming and handsome, but generous, fair-minded, wise, learned, the most lovable and popular king England had known in a century. Now, thirty years of physical and mental suffering—a good deal of the latter self-inflicted—had taken their toll. He was no longer easy to live with, and the old charm and generosity were only revealed in occasional flashes.

Henry remained blithely unaware that princesses all across Europe were pleading with their families not to send them to England. As far as he was concerned, Katherine and Anne had been to blame for their own sufferings, and Jane's death was no one's fault. Nonetheless, he paid court to at least one lady, the Duchess of Milan, who fairly laughed at the ambassador who approached her on Henry's behalf:

"...The King's Majesty was in so little space rid of the queens that she dare not trust his Council, though she durst trust his Majesty; for her council suspecteth that her great-aunt [Katherine of Aragon] was poisoned, that the second was innocently put to death, and the third lost for lack of keeping in her childbed."

If she had two heads, she continued, "one should be at his Grace's service!"

During this period, relations between England and Catholic Europe were deteriorating; for this reason, Thomas Cromwell advised Henry to "forget his religious scruples and ally himself to one of the Protestant German Princes, a move which he predicted would tip the balance of power in Europe in England's favor once more." Such an alliance might dissuade the Emperor, Charles V, from making an alliance with the King of France and attacking England to avenge past insults to Katherine and Mary. Cromwell suggested that Henry pay court to one of the daughters of the Duke of Cleves: either Anne, the second born (her older sister Sybilla was married already), or her younger sister Amelia. Though in later centuries all the royal houses of Europe would flock to the German principalities for their brides, never before had the daughter of a minor German house been considered as a potential Queen of England. The Duke of Cleves was overjoyed by the thought of making such a match for one of his daughters, the bridegroom's past marital history notwithstanding.

The short history of Henry VIII and Anne of Cleves

Henry had more than politics on his mind when it came to the selection of his fourth wife. Attractive, she must be, but not too small and slender, for "I am big in person, and need a big wife." He preferred women like Katherine and Jane, who were both plump and buxom, to women like Anne, who was petite and inclined to be thin—not a desirable feminine quality in the Tudor era. A few years before, Henry had made overtures to the French court, seeking a bride from one of the daughters of the royal family, or even a highborn lady—but he wanted them to travel to England so that he might see them in person first. King Francis found this almost too laughable too be insulting; royal marriages were never conducted in this manner, and he compared Henry to a horse breeder going to market. With this in mind, no one suggested that Lady Anne or Lady Amelia go to England, but Henry insisted on sending his favorite portrait painter, Hans Holbein, to Cleves to take their likenesses.

Anne and Amelia's father had recently died and the new Duke was their brother, a man with extremely strict notions of feminine modesty.

His sisters were required to move about in public so heavily cloaked and veiled that it was impossible to get any idea of their figure or their facial features. There were reports that Lady Anne was the more beautiful of the two sisters, but no one really knew for sure. Thomas Cromwell, who had suggested the Cleves marriage to Henry in the first place, made sure to have a private word with Holbein before he left England: Holbein was to be sure that Anne looked very good indeed in the portrait he painted of her. Cromwell's place in Henry's favor depended on the success of the Cleves marriage.

Additional pressure was placed on Holbein when Anne's brother told Henry that he was too poor to give her a dowry, that he was concerned how Anne would fare in a famously licentious court, given the strict, narrow religious principles of her upbringing, and that the fates of Henry's previous queens made him worry for Anne's safety. Henry, by now almost excessively eager for the marriage to take place, struck a bargain: he was king, and rich enough to take a bride even if she lacked a dowry. So long as he was pleased with what he saw in her portrait, he would take Anne to wife precisely as he found her.

In early November 1540, Anne left Cleves and traveled overland to Calais, where she was met by the Duke of Suffolk and the Earl of Southampton, whom Henry had appointed to escort her the rest of the way into England. She was supposed to join Henry by Christmas, enter London officially on January 1st, be married to him on January 6th, and be crowned Queen of England on February 2nd. However, stormy weather made passage across the English Channel impossible for several days, which meant that Anne would miss most of the Christmas festivities Henry had planned for her. Not until December 26th was Anne's retinue able to proceed to England; she arrived in Deal at 5 in the morning the following day. Despite a freezing winter storm, she pressed onwards towards London; breaking her journey at the Bishop's palace at Canterbury. Throughout her progress from Cleves to Canterbury, the English nobles in her retinue after had studied her thoroughly, considering the impression she made, trying to decide whether she would please the King. Anne was reported to be highly intelligent but she spoke no English, French, or Latin, only High Dutch, which no one at Henry's court spoke. Nonetheless, everyone agreed that her behavior was extremely pleasing, that she conducted herself like a true princess, that she was neither over-awed by the crowds of people gathering to see her nor insensible to the honor they paid her.

A handful of people reckoned her a beauty. The first person to contradict that report was Lady Browne, the capable matron who had been selected to manage the Queen's newly appointed maids of honor. Taking one look at Anne, Lady Browne "could barely conceal her dismay". It wasn't so much that Anne was ugly; but ladies of the English court had a certain way of dressing, of arranging their hair, of maintaining elegance in their person, that enhanced plain features or made them unnoticeable. Anne, brought up in a pious, nearly cloistered atmosphere where women were given very little freedom even by 16th century standards, had no such elegance, no such coiffure or style, and as a result, she looked very plain standing next to an English lady.

This, probably, accounts for Henry's reaction when he finally laid eyes on Anne, shortly after she arrived at the Bishop's palace. He was not supposed to meet her that night, but he was bursting with impatience to set eyes on his future wife after so many delays had kept him from her, so he rode out to the Bishop's palace in the late evening, catching them all by surprise—not unlike Henry VII had done in his impatience to examine the Spanish princess Katherine who had come to marry his son Arthur. Henry VII had been pleased with what he saw when he lifted the edges of Katherine's veil and saw the plump, pretty princess beneath. It is not certain what precisely Henry VIII saw when he was ushered into Anne's presence—but his reaction to her appearance is the most famously disastrous first meeting between intended lovers in history. As far as Henry was concerned, Holbein had flattered her outrageously in his portrait, and Cromwell had outright lied about her appearance.

Despite his disappointment, Henry behaved well during this first introduction. He graciously welcomed Anne to England and paid her all the tender compliments of a husband-to-be. But as soon as the audience was over, his temper flared. Sir Anthony Browne, wife of the perspicacious Lady Browne who had seen at a glance that Anne would never suit Henry's tastes, was waiting in the hallway. Henry told Sir Anthony that he was "so struck with consternation when he saw the Queen" that he had never been "so much dismayed in his life as to see a lady so far unlike what had been represented." He declared, "I see nothing in this woman as men report of her, and I marvel that wise men would make such report as they have done!"

Yet Henry was trapped. The betrothal contract was almost as binding as a marriage, and he felt he had no choice but to let the wedding arrangement proceed as they had been planned. Yet he was furious with Cromwell, who had got him into this mess, and Henry let him know that he expected him to find some means of extricating him from the marriage. But Cromwell, after claiming that he himself had been misled as to Anne's charms, stood his ground. He was convinced that England must have an alliance with Cleves, regardless of how disappointing the bride was. Furthermore, he pointed out to the King that Anne deserved better at his hands than to be rejected at this stage when she had done nothing to deserve it; no other king or prince would marry her if Henry cast her off now, and her prospects would be ruined. And her brother would probably declare war on Henry if Anne met with poor treatment at his hands.

As the weeks progressed and Henry saw more of Anne, his disappointment and his determination to be free of the marriage only grew more entrenched. With some coaxing from Cromwell, he agreed that Anne had a good figure and a queenly bearing, but it was not enough; Henry could not love her. "I like her not," he kept repeating. Yet he managed to behave with all outward courtesy towards Anne during the few occasions they saw each other before the wedding. On January 4, two days before the date set for the wedding, Henry declared that,

"If it were not that she had come so far into my realm, and the great preparations and state that my people have made for her, and for fear of making a ruffle in the world and of driving her brother into the arms of the Emperor and the French King, I would not now marry her. But now it is too far gone, wherefore I am sorry."

The marriage took place as scheduled, with Henry expressing his reluctant and apprehensions to all who attended upon him up to the very point of entering the church. After the wedding, and the banquets, and the marital entertainments, Henry and Anne retired to bed. As it happened, Anne's mother had neglected to fulfill that traditional duty of mothers towards daughters on the eve of their wedding—that is, she had failed to explain how marital relations work, and what she should expect from her husband in bed. So she was confused, but not offended, when the marriage was not consummated that night. The next morning, Cromwell earnestly inquired of the King how the wedding night had gone:

"Surely my lord," [said Henry], "I liked her before not well, but now I like her much worse! She is nothing fair, and have very evil smells about her. I took her to be no maid by reason of the looseness of her breasts and other tokens, which, when I felt them, strake me so to the heart, that I had neither will nor courage to prove the rest. I can have none appetite for displeasant airs. I have left her as good a maid as I found her."

From this point forward, there could be no doubt in Cromwell's mind: Henry was setting the groundwork for an annulment. Henry told everyone—his Privy Councilors, his courtiers, his doctor, etc—that he had been unable to consummate the marriage, not because he was impotent, but because Anne repelled him. Anne quickly became the butt of every kind of low joke; it is just as well that she spoke no English and could not be aware what people were saying about her. But she was beginning to understand enough of the language to communicate a little with her ladies in waiting. They listened as she described what went on when Henry visited her at night—he would greet her with a kiss, fall asleep, and take his leave of her in the morning. One of her ladies told her that this meant she was still a virgin; Anne was confused, thinking that virginity ceased to exist once a woman had lain all night in a bed with her husband. "Madam, there must be more than this," one of her ladies attempted to explain. But Anne declared that "she received quite as much of his Majesty's attention as she wished." One wonders if Anne had been as disappointed with Henry's appearance and physical attractions as he had been with hers.

Even as Henry was urging his advisors and councilors to find some pretext for divorcing or annulling his marriage to Anne, he was beginning to draw "too near another lady". This was Katherine Howard, one of Anne's ladies and the niece of the Duke of Norfolk. Katherine was about fifteen at the time; it is impossible to be certain of her exact age, since, like Anne Boleyn, there are no surviving records containing her precise date of birth. But she was known to be exceptionally young, a good ten years younger at least than any of Henry's previous wives, though by no means too young to marry by Tudor standards. Katherine was pretty, charming, naïve, and had long ago been seduced by the atmosphere of romantic intrigue at court. As her uncle Norfolk began to maneuver her closer to Henry, Katherine understood well that he hoped to make her Queen of England one day—and Katherine was probably too young to understand how dangerous a prospect this was, since she had been a young child during the days of Queen Katherine and the first Queen Anne. She was ambitious enough to think Henry an admirable suitor, even though he was by now middle-aged, fat, and stank continually because of the sore on his leg. And Henry was, as one historian points out, just at that age when men begin to feel especially flattered by the attentions of very young women, as though seeking assurance that they are still vigorous and in their sexual prime. He soon fell passionately in love with Katherine Howard, unaware that he was not the first man to sue for her affections.

In June of 1540, Henry had Cromwell arrested for treason and conducted to the Tower. Immediately after, he began making plans to annul his marriage to Anne. He had her conveyed to the palace at Richmond, claiming that there was plague in the city, and that he would join her within two days. When two days elapsed and Henry did not come, Anne began to realize that there was probably truth to the rumors about Henry's love affair with Katherine Howard. She was also clever enough to sense that her marriage was about to come to an end, but unlike Katherine of Aragon, she had no intention of fighting it. Her marriage to Henry had become as disagreeable to her as it was to him; she would be relieved to find herself free of it. When Henry sent a delegation of nobles to Anne to explain that he was instituting divorce proceedings against her, she said, "plainly and frankly that she was contented that the discussion of the matter be committed to the clergy as judges competent on that behalf." Henry was elated when news of her response was reported back to him. Anne was going to give him his way, which was what he wanted from women above all else. He would prove exceptionally kind and generous to Anne after their marriage ended, as an expression of gratitude for sparing him the trouble and pain of protracted legal proceedings.

On July 9th, 1540, the Bishops of Canterbury and York declared that Anne and Henry's marriage was null and void, owing to a pre-contract that existed between Anne and one of her former suitors, and to the fact that her union with Henry had not been consummated. Almost as quickly as the matter had been undertaken, it was completed. Henry sent another delegation to Anne at Richmond informing that the annulment had been declared, and "henceforth it was the King's pleasure that she call herself his sister", and that he was giving her an annual allowance of £4000 as well as several properties: Richmond, Bletchingly, and Hever Castle, Anne Boleyn's childhood home. On July 11, Anne wrote to Henry, saying that "though this case must needs be both hard and sorrowful for me, for the great love which I bear to your most noble person," she accepted the finding of the court, "whereby I neither can nor will repute myself your Grace's wife, considering this sentence and your Majesty's pure and clean living with me." But she hoped that sometimes she would behold his "most noble presence, which I shall esteem for a great benefit." She was flattered that "your Highness will take me for your sister, for the which I most humbly thank you accordingly."

Anne of Cleves sent word to her brother, Duke William, that she intended to spend the rest of her life in England, where she was now a single woman of immense property, enjoying a greater degree of freedom and independence than nearly any other woman who lived there. She would always enjoy high status, since, as the King's sister, she took precedence over everyone at court save the King's nearest blood relations. She was relieved to have escaped Henry with her life and her honor; the wealth and status she received as a reward for her compliance only sweetened the deal.

Chapter Six: Katherine Howard and Katherine Parr (1540-1547)

Katherine Howard, Queen of England

The short, unhappy life of Katherine Howard is perhaps the darkest chapter in the saga of Henry VIII and his six wives. She was destined to meet the same fate as Anne Boleyn, but at least in the case of Anne, who was so much older, cleverer, and more capable of making her own decisions, it is fair to judge that she knew the risks she was taking and was playing a game she knew might lose. Katherine, on the other hand, was "a frivolous, empty-headed young girl who cared for little else but dancing and pretty clothes"—in other words, a normal teenager. She, like all the Queens before her, was the pawn of her powerful male relatives, but more so than any of her predecessors, she was also their victim. Simply put, she was in over her head from the beginning, and it pleased her uncle and the King to put her in that position for their own selfish reasons—ambition, on Norfolk's part, and egocentric lust on Henry's. Katherine Howard was a pretty, kind-hearted girl, free with her affections, the product of a licentious court where flirtation and sexual intrigue were the chief pastime. She had no political awareness, and no ability to sense when the net was closing over her. She married Henry on July 28th, 1540, the same day that Thomas Cromwell was executed. Sixteen months later, on February 13th, 1542, she was executed for adultery and treason.

At first, it seemed to Henry that he had found a wife who united all the qualities he required in a woman to be pleasing to him: "beauty, charm, a pleasant disposition, obedience, and, he believed, virtue." There is little to say of Katherine and Henry's married life, save that nothing in her existence had prepared her for being elevated to the status of a Queen, and she spent most of her time reveling in the sumptuous clothing, jewels, and other presents that Henry delighted in bestowing upon her. Henry had hopes that Katherine would give him another son, but unlike Katherine of Aragon, Anne Boleyn, or Jane Seymour, all of whom became pregnant within a month or so of marrying Henry, Katherine Howard never showed any signs of pregnancy—probably because Henry's ill health made him less fertile than he had been in youth and early middle age.

In February of 1541, a year before Katherine's execution, Henry's ulcerated leg began to cause him a great deal of pain, and his temper became correspondingly vicious. He fell into a deep depression, and began shutting himself away for long periods of time. Only in the days immediately after Jane Seymour's death had he retreated from the public life of the court in such a fashion. Katherine was alarmed—she seems to have had enough native wit to understand that if the King was unhappy, he might well come to blame her for it, regardless of how hard she worked to please him. But he seems to have recovered his spirits somewhat by the end of the month, to Katherine's great relief.

Katherine's downfall began in late 1541, when a man by the name of John Lascelles informed Thomas Cranmer, Archbishop of Canterbury, that "he knew things about the Queen's past that would reflect upon her marriage with the King." Lascelles, like Cranmer, was a Protestant, while Katherine Howard, as the niece of the Duke of Norfolk, represented the interests of the Catholic faction at court. Cranmer, unlike other advisors Henry had depended on, such as Wolsey and Cromwell, was a man of integrity, without overt malice or cruelty; but he would not be sorry to see Katherine replaced by a Protestant Queen who would advance the cause of the Reformed church in England. So when Lascelles told him that his sister Mary had known Katherine before her marriage, and that she had proclaimed

Katherine to be "light, both in living and in conditions [i.e. behavior]", Cranmer took him seriously. Upon interviewing Lascelles' sister, Cranmer learned that Katherine had indulged in a serious flirtation with a common musician at the Duke of Norfolk's house, and had later had become the lover of Francis Dereham.

Cranmer, convinced that the woman was telling the truth, felt that he had a duty to inform Henry; any hint of impropriety in the Queen's character was a matter of national importance, because it might endanger the succession. Nonetheless, Henry was deeply in love with Katherine, and in his grief and anger he might lash out against Cranmer himself. Cranmer therefore wrote a letter, which he presented to Henry in November of 1541; Henry, reading it, declared that it could not be true, but that Cranmer was to make a thorough investigation, in order to clear Katherine's name. In the mean time, the Queen was to be confined to her chambers with only a single lady in waiting to look after her. Henry declared that he would not see her until she was proven innocent of all charges.

Henry never saw Katherine Howard again. For the next four months, from November of 1541 to

February of 1542, her conduct was investigated, and she was left to suffer in isolation and terror, for as soon as she was informed of the charges against her, she knew that she was destined to die a traitor's death. Even Cranmer, whose job it was to interrogate her, was stirred to pity. He found her "in such lamentation and heaviness as I never saw no creature, so that it would have pitied any man's heart in the world to have looked upon." Cranmer urged Katherine to write a full and free confession of every instance in which she had ever had any sexual knowledge of a man, telling her that the King wished to be merciful. This, Katherine did, and when Henry read the letter, he was cheered; it did not matter to him so much that his wife had had dalliances before her marriage, so long as she had not been unfaithful to him after they were married. Furthermore, Cranmer told Henry that he had found evidence of a marital pre-contract between Katherine and one of the men she was accused of sleeping with—such a contract would invalidate Katherine's marriage to Henry, making it possible for an annulment to be arranged. This was seen as the best possible outcome to a situation which Henry had feared would end with Katherine's head on the block. Monstrously selfish as Henry could be, he had no desire to execute another wife.

Cranmer, however, was determined to find evidence of adultery. He had no personal animosity against Katherine, but he wanted a Protestant Queen, and he was willing to sacrifice Katherine's life to that end. He was partially successful; Katherine had been flirting with, and writing to, one of Henry's courtiers, named Thomas Culpepper. A damning letter from Katherine to Culpepper was discovered, in which she signed herself "yours as long as life endures". This, combined with the testimony of some of Katherine's ladies that they had left Katherine and Culpepper alone together for long periods of time, was enough to condemn her, even though Culpepper insisted that they had never consummated their affair. There was no evidence that Katherine had ever had sexual relations with Culpepper, but having heard testimony as to her "light conduct" before marriage, Cranmer was convinced that adultery had taken place, and he shared this conviction with the King. Henry believed him. Katherine's fate was accordingly sealed.

Henry had initially been inclined to show mercy towards Katherine out of respect for her tender age and the love he bore her—he had long been out of love with Anne Boleyn when she was executed. But the evidence Cranmer presented him with provoked him into an absolute rage.

His love for Katherine was transmuted into hatred, and on one occasion he had "called for a sword to slay her he had loved her so much. Sitting in Council, he suddenly called for hoses without saying where he would go. Sometimes he will say irrelevantly that the wicked woman never had such delight in her incontinence as she should have torture in her death."

Parliament convened on January 16, 1542, and drew up a Bill of Attainder, formally asking the King for permission to convict "Mistress Katherine Howard, late Queen of England" of treason, punishable by death. When news of her condemnation was brought to Katherine, she received it like a girl who had matured considerably in a matter of months. She was calm and unsurprised, and made no attempt to defend herself. She declared that she wished only to make a dignified end; all she asked of the King was that her execution be conducted privately, not before an audience of commoners, as Anne Boleyn's had been. This request was granted. Katherine Howard was imprisoned in the Tower of London on February 10th, 1542, where she was executed, in the presence of the King's Council, on Monday, February 13th, at seven in the morning. One observer wrote later that she made a "godly and Christian end," asking "all Christian people to take regard unto her worthy and just punishment with death, for her offences against God heinously from her youth upward in breaking of all His commandments, and also against the King's Royal Majesty very dangerously." Moments later, Katherine Howard's head was struck from her body in a single blow of the axe.

Katherine Parr, Queen of England

Losing—or murdering—Katherine Howard had made an old man of Henry VIII at last. Not only had her sexual improprieties shattered his illusions that he remained a vigorous, desirable lover, attractive to women of all ages, but on some level it seems to have shamed him that he had taken possession of so young a girl, only to deliver her to such a brutal fate. Moreover, with the exception of the two years between the death of Jane Seymour and his marriage to Anne of Cleves, he had never, since he was eighteen years old, been without the company of a wife—that is, he had never got rid of one woman without having another waiting in the wings to step into her predecessor's place. But there was no one waiting to take Katherine Howard's place. Henry was burdened by a corpulent, failing body, agitated by physical pain and an unquiet conscience. His ministers wanted him to marry again, naturally—so long as there was a chance of providing Prince Edward with a brother, that chance must be seized. And men had fathered children at far more advanced ages than 51. But Henry was tired and dispirited. A full eighteen months would pass before his eye would settle on another woman who pleased him.

Katherine Parr was married when Henry first singled her out for attention, although her husband was ill and expected to die shortly. She was 31 years old, a distant descendant of King Edward III. She had been married at the age of 13 to a man "old enough to be her grandfather" whose identity is uncertain—his name is recorded as Lord Borough, which might refer to several men of the right age living at the time. Lord Borough died three years later, when Katherine was sixteen. With her parents and husband dead, Katherine was her own mistress, but she chose to accept a second offer of marriage two years later, to John Neville, Lord Latimer, who was in his thirties. As Lady Latimer, Katherine had often been to the court of Henry VIII, and they met a number of times during the years of her marriage. When Lord Latimer died on March 2, 1543, Katherine had already received a number of rich gifts from the King, gifts which made the nature of his interest in her impossible to misunderstand. Henry was certain that she would be flattered by his attentions, but she was not. She was deeply dismayed, because she was falling in love with the dashing Lord Thomas Seymour, brother of Queen Jane Seymour, and he was hinting of asking her to marry him. Though Seymour was a notorious ladies' man, the seriousness of his intentions towards Katherine Parr were proved when he married her less than a year after Henry VIII's death.

Compared to the handsome, athletic, relatively youthful Thomas Seymour, Henry was anything but an attractive suitor. He was aware that Seymour wanted Katherine; Seymour reminded him of himself as a younger man, and this kindled Henry's jealousy in several different ways. In the end, Henry trampled over Seymour's suit and proposed to Katherine Parr in July of 1543. Katherine, being only a private widow and not the daughter of a powerful lord or foreign monarch, did not have it in her power to refuse. A proposal of marriage from the King to one of his subjects was as good as a command. She tried to demur, but Henry became insistent, and at last she capitulated.

Katherine was past the first flush of youthful beauty, but her sobriety, maturity, erudition— she was the most highly educated of all Henry's wives, a formidable scholar and eventually a patron of universities—were qualities that attracted him to her. Being twice married and in her thirties, she had enough experience of the world to help her manage a difficult older husband and a treacherous royal court. Most importantly, her virtue was beyond question; no one would dream of suspecting her of affairs or youthful dalliances, as she had been contracted in honorable marriage at the same age that Katherine Howard was flirting with musicians in Lambeth.

Katherine Parr was a very popular Queen. She had administered large estates and knew how to manage households and look after her dependents, a skill set which translated admirably to fulfilling the duties of Henry's wife. She was pleasant, loved to engage in conversation and intellectual debate, and had a gentle manner that pleased everyone who met her. And, though Henry undoubtedly was not thinking along such lines when he chose her, she was a capable nurse who had cared for her first aged husband through a long illness when she was only a girl. Katherine Parr would not shrink from Henry's stinking, ulcerated leg sores, but would bathe them and dress them more capably than most doctors.

She did not wish to be Queen, but finding herself in that estate, she made up her mind to do her duty to her sovereign, her people, and to God. Even her intellect was put into the service of religion. She was the author of a treatise, *The Lamentations of a Sinner,* published in 1547. For all of these qualities, Henry respected her—his love for her was not passionate, but he esteemed her as much as he had esteemed Jane Seymour and probably regarded her abilities even more highly. Henry had married her chiefly for companionship, and in this light, he could not have chosen better. Henry's chancellor, Wriothesley, described Katherine Parr as

"a woman, in my judgement, for certain virtue, wisdom, and gentleness, most meet for his Highness. And sure I am that his Majesty had never a wife more agreeable to his heart than she is. The Lord grant them long life and much joy together."

One of Katherine's chief goals during her marriage to Henry was to be a loving stepmother to his three children. Mary and Elizabeth had been living apart from court from years, and even Edward spent most of his time at his own house. The King's three children saw little of their father and less of each other, and Katherine wished to rectify this. Mary had been good friends with both Jane Seymour and Anne of Cleves, though she had disliked Katherine Howard and never attempted to get to know her; Elizabeth visited Anne of Cleves occasionally, with Henry's permission, and she had been deeply affected by the death of Katherine Howard. In fact, it is thought to be Katherine Howard's execution which made Elizabeth resolve never to marry. Katherine wanted all of Henry's children to come to court where she could look after them, and she secured Henry's permission to issue the invitations in August of 1543, a month after the wedding. Mary and Elizabeth promptly came to wait on the new Queen. Elizabeth, who was now nearly ten, was now "as intelligent and sharp-witted as many an adult" and for this reason, or perhaps because she reminded him so much of her mother, Henry had never been entirely easy in her company. But under Katherine's influence, he softened towards her. Elizabeth was already a precocious scholar, which delighted the clever and erudite Queen, and Katherine decided to supervise Elizabeth's education personally. Mary, who was nearly the same age as Katherine, also came to consider the Queen a great friend, particularly because

Katherine was careful to ensure that Mary received all the deference due her status as the King's eldest daughter. Six-year old Edward came to court least often of the three children, due to the fact that Henry was terrified that too much time spent in London would expose him to some fatal malady. But he too became fond of Katherine, and even when he was away from court, the Queen did everything in her power to provide him with motherly supervision.

In the last two years of Henry's life, Katherine was to enjoy a less comfortable atmosphere at court. Anti-Protestant feeling was high, and Henry was persecuting "heretics" with vigor, including one Anne Askew, who was racked and burnt at the stake. There were a number of Protestants among Katherine's household, but she took great care never to outwardly identify herself as one, for fear of risking Henry's displeasure. But Henry's health problems were causing him so much suffering that he was displeased with things in general, and some of the qualities that had pleased him in Katherine before, like her taste for intellectual debate on matters of religion, began to irk him. He ceased visiting her apartments, and Katherine was never certain whether she should offer him her company after dinner or not.

Katherine, like most of the Queens before her, was to become the focus of political intrigue at court. The Catholic faction suspected her of sympathies towards the Protestants, and when Henry was seen to lose patience with Katherine after a theologically-themed conversation, a certain Bishop Gardiner seized his chance. He wished to paint Katherine as a heretic in Henry's eyes. He pointed out that,

"it was unseemly for any of his subjects to argue with him so malapertly as the Queen had just done; that it was grievous for any of his Councillors to hear it done, since those who were so bold in words would not scruple to proceed to acts of disobedience."

He added that,

"he could make great discoveries if he were not deterred by the Queen's powerful faction. Besides this, the religion by the Queen maintained did not only dissolve the politic government of princes, but also taught the people that all things out to be in common."

Gardiner was, effectively, not only trying to convince Henry that his wife was a heretic, but that she was at the center of a kind of anarchist conspiracy to end the rule of lawful government in England. Gardiner talked to the King on this subject for hours, and by the end, Henry authorized Gardiner to draw up charges of heresy against Katherine, though she was not immediately informed of this. In fact, Henry continued to debate theological matters with her, sounding her opinions for any evidence of the heresy Gardiner had accused her of.

Only by accident did Katherine escape the worst. A warrant for her arrest, bearing the King's signature, was carelessly dropped within sight of one of Katherine's servants, who immediately brought it to her. Katherine instantly perceived the meaning; she saw that she was destined for an even worse fate than Anne Boleyn and Katherine Howard. They had only been executed for sexual indiscretions; the punishments meted out to heretics were far worse. She instantly had a panic attack, crying and screaming, her lamentations echoing throughout the chambers of the palace. Henry, having no idea what was wrong with her, ordered his doctors to attend her. Later, he came to visit her himself. He found his normally composed, self-controlled wife in an absolutely broken state. Only with difficulty did

Katherine manage to tell him that she was afraid she had incurred his displeasure and lost his love. Henry, moved by her obvious grief, "like a loving husband, with comfortable words so refreshed her careful mind that she began somewhat to recover."

Katherine had received a stay from her ordeal, but she knew that she was not entirely out of danger yet. She made use of the reprieve to gather her wits and devise a strategy to allay any suspicion Henry might be entertaining regarding her heretical leanings, or her desire to influence him for the Protestant cause. That night, when Henry invited Katherine to dispute with him on the subject of religion once more, she avoided the trap by saying that, as God had made Henry head of the Church of England, it was his opinions that truly mattered. "Not so, by St. Mary!" Henry persisted. "Ye are become a doctor, Kate, to instruct us, as oftentime we have seen, and not to be instructed or directed by us." This was the opening Katherine had been waiting for: she immediately began to explain that she had only ever debated religion with him because she knew it helped to

"pass away the pain and weariness of your present infirmity, which encouraged me in this boldness, in the hope of profiting withal by your Majesty's learned discourse. I am but a woman, with all the imperfections natural to the weakness of my sex; and therefore in all matters of doubt and difficulty I must refer myself to your Majesty's better judgment, as to my lord and head."

It was a speech precisely calculated to soothe Henry's affronted feelings and divert him from a course that would have spelled disaster for Katherine. "Is it so, sweetheart?" he asked, both relieved and impressed. "And tended your arguments to no worse end? Then we are perfect friends, as ever at any time heretofore." He kissed her in the presence of all his courtiers and told her that "it did him more good to hear those words from her own mouth than if he had heard news of £100,000 coming his way. Never again, he promised, would he doubt her." When Chancellor Wriothesley came to arrest Katherine with forty of the king's guard the next day, he found her in Henry's company, and Henry as pleased with his Queen as he had ever been in his life. Henry fell into a fury with his Chancellor, calling him a beast and a knave, and sent him on his way. Katherine knew, of course, that Wriothesley had come to arrest her, but she pretended to know nothing. For the rest of Henry's life, she would hide the keenness of her intellect from him. It was not safe for a Queen to be too much herself in the King's presence; this was a lesson Katherine had intuited from the examples of her predecessors.

By the following year, 1546, Henry was aware that he could not live much longer. He was extremely ill by Christmas, and there were no public festivities at the court; only his Privy Council, Katherine, and his daughter Mary kept him company over the holiday. The illness stemmed from his leg, and the sore which had plagued him since he was a young man. It was infected again, and he was running a high fever. On December 30, he dictated his will, ordering the line of succession: the crown would pass first to his only son, Prince Edward, now nine years old. If Edward died without issue, the throne would go to any child which Katherine might bear Henry after his death. His daughter Mary and her heirs were next in line, then his daughter Elizabeth and her heirs, then the heirs of his late sister Mary, Frances Brandon and her daughter, Lady Jane Grey. He also made provisions for Katherine's widowhood, bestowing £3000 worth of household items and jewels for her use in her lifetime, in acknowledgment of "the great love, obedience, chastity of life and wisdom being in our wife and Queen."

On his deathbed, Henry called Katherine to him, to say his final farewell to the wife who would outlive him. "It is God's will that we should part," he began, then gestured to the members of his Privy Council, standing nearby:

"I order all these gentlemen to treat you as if I were living still, and if it should be your pleasure to marry again, I order that you shall have £7000 for your service as long as you live, and all your jewels and ornaments."

Coming from Henry, this was a stunningly magnanimous gesture, and Katherine was deeply affected by it. She had not wanted to marry Henry in the first place, but she had come to feel a deep, if complicated affected for the complicated King who had chosen her, and she could not help weeping at the thought of losing him.

Henry VIII died at two in the morning on January 28, 1547, too weak, in the end, to utter the words of his final confession, but strong enough to give Archbishop Cranmer a sign that he "put his trust in God, through Jesus Christ." He was fifty-five years old. In compliance with his instructions, he was interred alongside the body of his third queen, Jane Seymour. When the funeral procession conveyed his body to its final resting place, the banners of Jane Seymour and Katherine Parr were seen in the cortege. In the end, they were the only two Queens whom Henry acknowledged as true wives.

Katherine Parr died on September 5, 1548. Six months after the death of Henry VIII, Katherine married her old friend, Thomas Seymour, in secret. At the age of 35, she became pregnant for the first time in her life, though this was her fourth marriage. The child, a girl called Mary, was born on August 30th, 1548. Katherine succumbed to puerperal fever a week later, dying as Jane Seymour died, nineteen months after the death of the man they had both called husband.

Other great books by Michael W. Simmons on Kindle, paperback and audio:

Elizabeth I: Legendary Queen Of England

Alexander Hamilton: First Architect Of The American Government

William Shakespeare: An Intimate Look Into The Life Of The Most Brilliant Writer In The History Of The English Language

Thomas Edison: American Inventor

Catherine the Great: Last Empress of Russia

Romanov: The Last Tsarist Dynasty

Peter the Great: Autocrat and Reformer

The Rothschilds: The Dynasty and the Legacy

Queen Victoria: Icon of an Era

Further Reading

The Six Wives of Henry VIII by Alison Weir

Defense of the Seven Sacraments, by Henry VIII

https://archive.org/details/cu319240293
98223

Katherine Parr, by Brandon G. Withrow

http://www.wtsbooks.com/common/pdf
links/9781596381179.pdf

"Whoso list to hunt", by Thomas Wyatt

https://www.poetryfoundation.org/poem
s-and-poets/poems/detail/45593

47575422R00106

Made in the USA
Middletown, DE
28 August 2017